the ski country cookbook

the ski country cookbook

barbara scott-goodman • photographs by rita maas

CHRONICLE BOOKS

SAN FRANCISCO

Library of Congress Cataloging-in-Publication Data available.
ISBN 978-0-8118-5977-6
Manufactured in China.

Art Direction and Design: Barbara Scott-Goodman
Food Styling: Michael Pederson
Prop Styling: Phyllis Asher

10 9 8 7 6 5 4 3 2 1

Chronicle Books LLC
680 Second Street
San Francisco, California 94107

www.chroniclebooks.com

contents

introduction

For most people, heading to ski country is a pure winter delight. Being high up in the majestic snow-covered mountains under crystal blue skies and puffy white clouds gives a sense of fresh revelation and well-being. Partaking of winter sports—downhill or cross-country skiing, snowboarding, snow-shoeing, sledding, or ice-skating—in fresh, cold white snow is exhilarating. These activities in the crisp, frosty weather are sure to stimulate our appetites.

The combination of cold mountain air and vigorous activity naturally makes us crave warm and restorative food. *The Ski Country Cookbook* is full of delicious, uncomplicated recipes that are a pleasure to prepare, serve, and eat, and that will surely satisfy those cravings. These recipes emphasize the goodness of hearty cold-weather food and are crafted for people who enjoy communing with nature during the day but who love to cook, eat, and socialize well into the night.

The hearty, stick-to-your-ribs fare featured in this book not only energizes you in the morning and sustains you during the day, it also recharges you in the evening, with both the joy of the preparation and the pleasure of eating. These lusty and earthy dishes are not at all pretentious or complicated. This is food that appeals to everyone—whether a family with their own ski house in Vail, weekend "snowbirds" heading to the White Mountains of New Hampshire, or a large group of twentysomething snow-boarders renting a vacation share in Tahoe.

On blustery winter mornings, you may want to fuel up on delicious homemade pancakes, frittatas, hash browns, or oatmeal before hitting the slopes or heading out for a long winter hike through the just-fallen snow. And after a day of schussing through powder, downhilling mountain trails, or cross-country skiing deep in the silences of snow-covered woods, there's nothing more satisfying than coming in from the cold and guiltlessly enjoying a warm and robust meal. In the chilly heart of ski country, substantial dishes—slow-simmering soups and stews, braised ribs and roasts, spicy chilis, make-your-own tacos, hearty pasta dishes accompanied by savory salads and side dishes—are just the right foods to serve for dinner. First, though, you may want to kick back and relax with a warm or cold après-ski cocktail and a few tasty appetizers in front of the fire. To follow all this robust fare, simple comfort-food desserts, such as pound cake, bread pudding, and homemade cookies and brownies, are sure to please everyone gathered at the table.

This is relaxed and simple winter dining at its best. Its style of cooking isn't demanding. Its ingredients aren't exotic—they come straight from the local market. This is hearty, warm, and delicious fare, made with a great sense of fun and generosity. Welcome to *The Ski Country Cookbook*.

chapter 1

breakfasts

freshly baked scones and muffins, homemade pancakes and frittatas, granola and oatmeal made from scratch—such is the heartwarming fare you crave on frosty winter mornings. This chapter offers a delightful array of breakfast treats for you to make for family and friends, whether you're whipping up an early breakfast before hitting the slopes or preparing a meal for a leisurely weekend. These hearty and delicious recipes are easy to prepare but so soul-warming, they'll keep you going all morning.

spicy hash browns & scrambled eggs

serves 6

Even if you're high in the North Country, you can draw inspiration from south of the border. Get a chilly day off to a hot start with a big breakfast of scrumptious hash-brown potatoes spiked with spicy paprika and cayenne, and scrambled eggs served with salsa on the side.

5 medium russet potatoes
2 tablespoons vegetable oil
1 tablespoon unsalted butter
1 onion, diced
1 clove garlic, thinly sliced

2 teaspoons garlic salt
½ teaspoon cayenne pepper
½ teaspoon hot paprika
Kosher salt and freshly ground black pepper
12 eggs
Salsa for serving (optional)

1. Bring a large pot of water to a boil and add the potatoes. Lower the heat and simmer until just tender, about 15 minutes. Drain and let cool. Skin the potatoes and cut into ½-inch dice.

2. In a large skillet, heat the oil and melt the butter over medium-high heat. Add the onion and garlic and cook, stirring, for 3 minutes. Add the potatoes, garlic salt, cayenne pepper, paprika, and salt and pepper to taste and cook, stirring gently, until the potatoes begin to turn brown and crisp, about 10 minutes.

3. In another skillet, prepare scrambled eggs to taste. Serve the eggs and hash browns with salsa, if desired.

vegetable frittata

serves 6 to 8

Frittatas are a fun and easy alternative to omelets to whip up for breakfast. This version is good served warm from the oven or at room temperature. Either way, serve with lots of hot toast and steaming mugs of coffee to chase away the morning chill.

½ tablespoon unsalted butter, plus more for the pan

8 eggs, at room temperature

¾ cup whole milk

1 plum tomato, finely diced

½ cup finely diced ham

½ cup freshly grated Gruyère cheese

¼ cup minced fresh chives

Kosher salt and freshly ground black pepper

½ cup diced shiitake mushrooms

¼ cup freshly grated Parmesan cheese

1. Preheat the oven to 350°F and butter a 9-by-12-inch baking pan or dish.
2. In a large bowl, whisk together the eggs and milk until well combined. Add the tomato, ham, Gruyère, chives, and salt and pepper to taste and whisk again.
3. Heat the butter in a small skillet and sauté the mushrooms until nicely browned, about 5 to 7 minutes. Whisk into the egg mixture.
4. Pour the mixture into the prepared pan and sprinkle to top with Parmesan cheese. Bake until the top of the frittata is firm and lightly browned, about 25 minutes. Serve warm or at room temperature.

smoked chicken & apple hash

serves 6 to 8

For a sensational hearty breakfast, serve this succulent hash with poached or scrambled eggs. The smoky flavor and crispy texture are perfect foils for the creamy eggs, and the combination will send you into the crisp morning air well satisfied.

4 red potatoes, unpeeled and cut into ½-inch dice

1 tablespoon unsalted butter

1 tablespoon olive oil

2 cloves garlic, thinly sliced

1 cup finely chopped onion

1 fennel bulb, cut into ½-inch dice

1 stalk celery, cut into ½-inch dice

2 Granny Smith apples, cored and cut into 1-inch chunks

6 ounces white mushrooms, stemmed and thinly sliced

2 smoked whole chicken breasts (about 2 pounds), boned and cut into 1-inch chunks (about 3½ cups)

Kosher salt and freshly ground black pepper

½ cup chopped fresh flat-leaf parsley

1. Bring a pot of lightly salted water to a boil. Boil the potatoes until just tender, 10 to 15 minutes. Drain and set aside.

2. In a large nonstick skillet, heat the butter and oil over medium-high heat. Add the garlic, onion, fennel, and celery and cook for about 5 minutes, stirring occasionally. Add the apples and mushrooms and cook for an additional 5 minutes.

3. Add the chicken pieces and cooked potatoes. Season to taste with salt and pepper. Cook over medium heat, turning occasionally with a spatula, until the hash is cooked through and slightly crusted. Stir in the parsley and taste and adjust the seasonings, if necessary. Serve immediately.

cornmeal pancakes
with fresh blueberry sauce

serves 4 to 6

Fresh pancakes are always a winter favorite, but when you're eager to hit the slopes, they can seem too time-consuming. These delicious corn cakes are great for the weekend cook because both the batter and sauce may be prepared well ahead of time. The blueberry sauce is also wonderful with ice cream or frozen yogurt.

BLUEBERRY SAUCE:

1¼ cups water

½ cup sugar

1 tablespoon fresh lemon juice

1 teaspoon cornstarch

2 cups fresh blueberries

1½ tablespoons currant jelly

PANCAKES:

1½ cups flour

2 tablespoons sugar

1 teaspoon baking powder

Kosher salt

½ cup cornmeal

2 eggs

1½ cups milk

Corn or safflower oil, for cooking

1. To prepare the blueberry sauce, combine the water, sugar, lemon juice, and cornstarch in a large saucepan and bring to a boil, stirring constantly to dissolve the sugar and cornstarch. Add the blueberries and jelly and bring to a boil. Reduce the heat to medium-low and simmer, stirring frequently, until the mixture is slightly thickened and reduced, about 30 minutes. Serve warm or at room temperature.

2. To prepare the pancakes, mix the flour, sugar, baking powder, and a pinch of salt together in a large bowl, and set aside.

continued

3. In a small saucepan, combine the cornmeal with 1½ cups water and a pinch of salt. Whisk until smooth while bringing to a boil over medium heat, then continue to stir for 5 minutes. Remove from the heat and let cool.
4. Beat the eggs into the cornmeal until smooth. Add to the flour mixture and stir to combine. Gradually stir in the milk until the batter is very smooth.
5. Heat 2 tablespoons of the oil over medium heat in a large skillet. When hot, add 2 to 3 tablespoons of the batter for each pancake with a large spoon. Cook until lightly browned on the bottom, about 2 minutes, then turn and brown second side. Repeat, using more oil. Serve warm with blueberry sauce.

Note: The sauce may be made up to 3 days ahead. Simply cover and chill. The batter may also be made ahead of time. It will keep, covered in the refrigerator, overnight. In the morning, bring to room temperature and mix well before cooking.

cranberry & toasted walnut muffins

makes 12 muffins

When you just can't wait to strap on your snowboard but still need to provide some tasty sustenance, pile these muffins in a basket and put them on the kitchen counter alongside a pot of hot fresh-brewed coffee. They won't stick around very long, either.

¼ pound (1 stick) unsalted butter, melted, plus more for the tin

2 cups unbleached all-purpose flour

2 teaspoons baking powder

½ teaspoon baking soda

½ teaspoon salt

1 cup frozen cranberries, thawed

½ cup walnut halves, toasted (see page 25)

½ cup sugar

½ cup light brown sugar

½ cup milk

1 large egg, lightly beaten

1 teaspoon vanilla extract

1. Preheat the oven to 400°F. Lightly butter a 12-muffin tin or line the tin with paper liners.
2. In a large bowl, whisk together the flour, baking powder, baking soda, and salt.
3. Put the cranberries, walnuts, sugar, and brown sugar in a food processor. Pulse 8 to 10 times until coarsely ground. Or, finely chop the cranberries and walnuts and toss them with the sugars.
4. In a medium bowl, combine the butter, milk, egg, and vanilla. Pour into the flour mixture and stir until just combined. Scrape the cranberry-walnut mixture into the batter and mix until just combined. Do not overmix.
5. Spoon the batter into the muffin cups, filling each one about two-thirds full. Bake for 15 to 20 minutes until the muffins are risen and browned and a tester inserted in the center comes out clean.
6. Set the muffin tins on wire racks to cool for about 5 minutes.

apricot & pecan scones

makes 8 to 10 scones

These rich and delicious scones can be assembled and baked in no time, and the aroma of baking scones on a chilly morning is heavenly. They're also wonderful to serve with tea in the afternoon.

2 cups unbleached all-purpose flour

¼ cup packed light brown sugar

1 tablespoon baking powder

Pinch of salt

½ cup dried apricots, finely chopped

¼ cup finely chopped pecans

1 cup heavy cream

¼ cup milk

1 large egg white, lightly beaten

1 to 2 teaspoons sugar

1. Preheat the oven to 425°F. Spray a baking sheet with vegetable-oil spray or line with parchment paper.
2. In a large bowl, whisk together the flour, brown sugar, baking powder, and salt. Add the apricots and pecans. Slowly stir in the cream and milk to form a sticky dough.
3. Turn the dough out onto a well-floured surface and, using a lightly floured rolling pin, roll it into a 9-inch circle about ¾-inch thick.
4. Stamp out the scones using a 2- or 2½-inch biscuit cutter or an overturned glass. Put the scones on the prepared baking sheet spaced about 1 inch apart.
5. Brush the tops of the scones with egg white and sprinkle with sugar. Bake until golden brown, about 15 to 20 minutes. Serve warm or at room temperature.

homemade granola

makes about 6 cups

Homemade granola is delicious as a breakfast cereal and also makes a great healthy snack to take with you hiking, sledding, or skiing. Its old-fashioned goodness will keep you going all day. Making your own couldn't be easier, and you can tailor it to your personal taste by adjusting the sweetness and the types and amounts of nuts and dried fruits.

3 cups rolled oats
1 cup unsweetened coconut
½ cup corn, canola, or safflower oil
½ cup chopped walnuts
½ cup sliced almonds
½ cup green pumpkin seeds
⅓ cup packed light brown sugar
2 tablespoons honey

Pinch of cinnamon
Pinch of salt
½ cup dried cherries
½ cup dried cranberries
½ cup dried blueberries
½ cup golden raisins
½ cup finely diced dried apricots

1. Preheat the oven to 325°F.
2. In a large bowl, stir the oats, coconut, oil, walnuts, almonds, pumpkin seeds, brown sugar, honey, cinnamon, and salt until well combined and evenly coated.
3. Spread the mixture evenly in a 10-by-14-inch shallow baking pan and bake, stirring occasionally, until golden brown, 25 to 30 minutes. Remove and let cool, stirring the granola occasionally, about 30 minutes. Stir in the dried fruit.

oatmeal with orange marmalade & toasted pecans

serves 6

Steel-cut oatmeal, also known as Irish or Scottish oatmeal, takes longer to cook than rolled oats or instant oatmeal, but its nutty flavor and chewy texture are well worth the time.

Steel-cut oatmeal, cooked according to package directions, to serve six

6 tablespoons orange marmalade

6 tablespoons toasted pecans, chopped (see below)

Warm milk, for serving

Divide the cooked oatmeal among 6 cereal bowls. Top each serving with a tablespoon each of marmalade and pecans. Serve at once with warm milk.

toasting nuts

Here are two easy methods for toasting nuts. Whichever one you use, watch the nuts carefully because they tend to burn quickly.

OVEN METHOD: Spread nuts on a baking sheet and toast in a preheated 350°F oven or toaster oven for about 5 minutes, until golden brown and fragrant. Shake the baking sheet once or twice during heating for even toasting. Slide the nuts off the baking sheet as soon as they reach the desired color, to halt the cooking. Let cool.

SKILLET METHOD: Warm the skillet over medium heat, add the nuts, and stir or shake the pan frequently, until they just begin to brown and are fragrant, 2 to 3 minutes. Remove from the heat, slide them on the a plate, and let cool. This method works well for a small quantity.

chapter 2

aprés-ski
appetizers

appetizers, munchies, or tapas—whatever you like to call them, plates of tasty snacks and trays of refreshing or warming drinks say "welcome" to your guests in a most pleasant way. Offer a variety of these easy-to-make nibbles along with a festive winter drink or a cheering glass of wine or beer in front of a roaring fire, and get the evening off to a terrific start.

sweet & spicy roasted nuts

Makes 4 cups

These toasted nuts are a sure-fire hit for a chilly ski weekend, and they may be made up to a week ahead of time, so you can keep plenty on hand. They're delicious to nibble on accompanied with cool cocktails.

Corn or canola oil, for brushing
   baking sheets
2 cups (½ pound) pecans
2 cups (½ pound) almonds
1 egg white
2 teaspoons chili powder
1 teaspoon ground cumin

½ teaspoon ground coriander
½ teaspoon ground cinnamon
½ teaspoon cayenne pepper
Freshly ground black pepper
2 tablespoons sugar
Kosher salt

1. Preheat the oven to 350°F. Lightly oil 2 baking sheets.
2. Put the pecans and almonds in a large bowl.
3. In a small bowl, beat the egg white until foamy. Pour over the nuts and toss to coat evenly.
4. Combine the chili powder, cumin, coriander, cinnamon, cayenne pepper, and black pepper to taste in a small skillet. Cook the spices, stirring constantly, until fragrant, about 3 minutes. Remove from the heat and stir in the sugar and salt to taste.
5. Add the spice mixture to the nuts and toss well to coat thoroughly.
6. Divide the nuts evenly between the baking sheets and spread in one layer. Bake for 15 minutes, shaking the pans every 5 minutes. Let cool. The nuts will keep in airtight containers for up to one week.

lemon-scented olives

serves 6 to 8; makes 2 cups

Here is an excellent way to prepare olives—sauté them in olive oil over low heat with slices of fresh lemon peel and herbs. When olives are warm, they taste rich and meaty, perfect for easing the chill of ski-country evenings.

1 tablespoon olive oil

2 cloves garlic, thinly sliced

2 cups mixed olives

1 teaspoon fresh lemon juice

Twelve ½-inch pieces lemon peel

1 teaspoon chopped fresh rosemary

1 teaspoon chopped fresh thyme

Freshly ground black pepper

Pinch of red pepper flakes, optional

Heat the oil in a skillet and sauté the garlic over medium heat until softened, about 2 minutes. Add the olives, lemon juice, lemon peel, rosemary, thyme, black pepper, and red pepper flakes, if using. Simmer, stirring occasionally, until heated through, about 10 minutes. Serve warm.

cider-braised chorizo bites

serves 4 to 6; makes 32 pieces

Spanish chorizo sausage used to be hard to find, but it is now widely available in a variety of markets. When these spicy sausages are braised in apple cider, they make a perfect small bite to serve by the fireside, along with warm olives and a glass of wine. Warning: These are irresistible, so you may want to double the recipe.

1 tablespoon olive oil

3 garlic cloves, thinly sliced

3 links (½ to ¾ pound) chorizo sausage, cut on the diagonal into ½-inch pieces

½ cup apple cider

Pinch of red pepper flakes

Freshly ground black pepper

1. Heat the olive oil in a medium skillet and sauté the garlic over medium heat until golden, about 2 minutes. Add the chorizo and sauté about 2 minutes.
2. Add the cider, red pepper flakes, and black pepper to taste and bring to a boil. Reduce the heat and simmer, stirring occasionally, until the cider is reduced by half, about 10 minutes.
3. Transfer to a platter and serve warm, with toothpicks.

roasted plum tomato salsa

makes 1¾ to 2 cups

In the summer, I love to make salsa from just-picked fresh tomatoes. But those delicious tomatoes are hard to come by during the winter. A tasty idea for bringing the warmth of summer to your winter gatherings is to use oven-roasted plum tomatoes. This salsa is great as a dip with tortilla chips or as a sauce to accompany scrambled eggs or roast chicken.

4 ripe plum tomatoes,
    coarsely chopped

2 tablespoons olive oil

Kosher salt and freshly ground
    black pepper

2 scallions (white and green parts),
    trimmed and minced

¼ cup chopped red onion

¼ cup chopped red bell pepper

1 tablespoon fresh lime juice

½ teaspoon ground cumin

½ teaspoon chili powder

1. Preheat the oven to 350°F.
2. Put the tomatoes, 1 tablespoon of the olive oil, and salt and pepper to taste in a large roasting pan and toss together. Roast the tomatoes, stirring occasionally, until tender, about 45 minutes. Remove from the oven and let cool.
3. Meanwhile, put the remaining 1 tablespoon of olive oil, the scallions, onion, bell pepper, lime juice, cumin, and chili powder in a medium bowl and toss together.
4. Transfer the tomatoes to a cutting board and chop. Add the tomatoes and their juices to the onion and pepper mixture and toss well. Taste and adjust the seasonings, adding more salt and pepper, if necessary. Serve chilled or at room temperature.

chicken, cheese, &
black bean nachos

serves 6

This hearty nacho recipe is a good snack to serve to hungry friends coming in from the wintry cold. It's fun to serve as finger food, eaten right out of the baking dish; it also makes a satisfying main course when served with rice and a salad.

2 cups (about ½ pound) shredded cooked chicken meat

2 tablespoons fresh lime juice

Kosher salt and freshly ground black pepper

3 tablespoons vegetable oil

2 red bell peppers, stemmed, seeded, and finely chopped

1 jalapeño pepper, stemmed, seeded, and finely diced

1 garlic clove, finely diced

1 teaspoon ground cumin

1 teaspoon chili powder

1 can (15.5 ounces) black beans, drained and rinsed

6 ounces yellow or blue corn tortilla chips

2 cups (½ pound) grated Monterey Jack cheese

¼ cup chopped scallions

½ cup chopped fresh cilantro

Hot sauce, for serving (optional)

Salsa, for serving (optional)

1. Preheat the oven to 375°F.
2. In a medium bowl, toss the chicken, lime juice, and salt and pepper to taste together and set aside.
3. In a large skillet, heat 2 tablespoons of the oil over medium heat. Sauté the bell and jalapeño peppers until crisp-tender, about 5 minutes. Transfer to a small bowl. Heat the remaining tablespoon of oil in the same skillet over medium heat and cook the garlic, cumin, and chili powder, stirring, about 2 minutes. Stir in the beans and cook, stirring, until heated through, about 3 minutes.

4. In a shallow 3-quart baking dish or casserole, layer one half of the chips, pepper mixture, beans, chicken, and cheese. Repeat layering with the remaining chips, pepper mixture, beans, chicken, and cheese. Stir the scallions and cilantro together and sprinkle over the top. Bake until the cheese is melted, 10 to 12 minutes. Serve with hot sauce and salsa, if desired.

crostini

Crostini are grilled or lightly baked toasts that are topped with spreads, cheese, meat, or vegetables on their own or in any combination. They are excellent to serve at big cocktail parties or small get-togethers. I've included ideas for hearty toppings that are especially fitting for the fireside (pages 38 to 40).

1 baguette or loaf of ciabatta bread, cut on the diagonal into ½-inch slices	1 large clove of garlic, peeled and cut in half Extra-virgin olive oil, for drizzling or brushing

GRILL METHOD: In a grill pan, grill the bread on both sides until nicely browned. While still hot, rub each slice gently with the cut side of the garlic and drizzle with olive oil. Serve with desired toppings.

OVEN METHOD: Preheat the oven to 350°F. Rub one side of the bread with the cut side of the garlic and brush both sides with olive oil. Arrange slices on 2 baking sheets. Bake until slightly dry on top, about 5 minutes. Turn and continue baking until crisp and golden brown, about 5 minutes. Serve with desired toppings.

gorgonzola & walnut spread

makes about 1½ cups or enough spread for 36 crostini

One 8-ounce package cream cheese, at room temperature, quartered

1 cup (¼ pound) Gorgonzola cheese, at room temperature

2 tablespoons heavy cream

¼ cup coarsely chopped walnuts

2 teaspoons cognac or brandy

Toasted walnut halves, for garnish

1. Put the cream cheese, Gorgonzola cheese, and heavy cream in a food processor and blend until smooth. Transfer to a mixing bowl and fold in the walnuts and cognac or brandy. Cover and refrigerate until chilled or up to 2 days.

2. Top warm crostini with the spread, garnish with walnut halves, and serve.

more crostini toppings

roasted fennel & chopped black olives

roasted zucchini & parmesan cheese

sautéed swiss chard & prosciutto

sautéed swiss chard & warm white beans

sautéed spinach & ricotta cheese

sautéed watercress & ham

sautéed broccoli rabe & mozzarella cheese

mozzarella cheese & anchovies

ricotta cheese, chopped tomatoes, & basil

brie cheese & fig jam

cheese fondue

If you wanted to host a party in the 1960s or 1970s, a fondue pot was a must, presenting a casual alternative to formal dining. It's still a cool and fun option for serving a crowd, and its Alpine ski chalet associations make it a natural in this setting. Offer an assortment of bite-size dipping foods, such as chunks of French and pumpernickel breads topped with paper-thin slices of ham or blanched or roasted vegetables. Spear with long wooden skewers or fondue forks, dip, swirl, and eat!

1 clove garlic, halved crosswise

1 cup dry white wine

2 cups (½ pound) Swiss cheese, coarsely grated

2 cups (½ pound) Gruyère cheese, coarsely grated

1 tablespoon cornstarch

1 tablespoon cherry brandy, such as kirsch

1 tablespoon fresh lemon juice

½ teaspoon dry mustard

Pinch of nutmeg

Accompaniments such as cubes of bread, ham slices, blanched or roasted asparagus, broccoli, carrots, cauliflower, and bell peppers

1. Rub the inside of a large heavy soup pot with cut sides of garlic and discard the garlic. Add the wine to the pot and bring to a low simmer over medium heat.
2. Gradually add the cheeses to the pot and cook, stirring constantly, until they are just melted and creamy; do not let boil.
3. In a small bowl, whisk together the cornstarch, brandy, lemon juice, mustard, and nutmeg until well blended and stir into the fondue. Bring the fondue to a simmer and cook, stirring, until thickened, 5 to 8 minutes.
4. Transfer to a fondue pot set over a flame and serve with accompaniments for dipping.

grilled cheese bites

makes 4 sandwiches; 16 pieces

It's hard to beat warm and comforting grilled cheese sandwiches made with slices of American, cheddar, or Monterey Jack cheese. When cooking for kids, I like to cut them up into bite-size pieces for snacks. Although a cast-iron skillet is a traditional favorite for making these sandwiches, a nonstick skillet is a better choice because the bread can stick to the bottom of a cast-iron pan and burn.

8 slices sandwich bread
 (¼-inch thick)
2 tablespoons unsalted butter,
 at room temperature

4 slices American, cheddar, or
 Monterey Jack cheese

1. Butter one side of each slice of bread. Put 4 slices, buttered side down, on a work surface. Put 1 slice of cheese over each of the 4 bread slices. Put the remaining 4 bread slices on top, buttered side up.
2. Heat a large nonstick skillet. Put the sandwiches in the skillet (in batches if necessary), cover, and cook until golden brown and the cheese has begun to melt, about 2 minutes. Turn the sandwiches with a spatula, and press to flatten them slightly. Cook until golden brown and the cheese has melted completely, about 1 minute. Cut each sandwich into quarters and serve at once.

grilled goat cheese & pesto mini-sandwiches

makes 4 sandwiches; 16 pieces

For more sophisticated après-ski settings, simple grilled cheese sandwiches, as satisfying as they are, may not suffice. These "grilled cheese for grown-ups" mini-sandwiches make savory, hearty appetizers or a tasty lunch. They can also be made with bruschetta, chunky salsa, tapenade, or artichoke spread instead of pesto sauce.

8 slices Italian country-style, sourdough, or olive bread (¼-inch thick)

2 tablespoons unsalted butter, at room temperature

¼ cup pesto sauce

6 tablespoons chopped sun-dried tomatoes

½ cup crumbled goat cheese

1. Butter one side of each slice of bread. Put 4 slices, buttered side down, on a work surface. Spread the pesto and tomatoes evenly over the 4 slices. Sprinkle the goat cheese over each of the 4 bread slices. Put the remaining 4 bread slices on top, buttered side up.

2. Heat a large nonstick skillet. Put the sandwiches in the skillet (in batches if necessary), cover, and cook until golden brown and the cheese has begun to melt, about 3 minutes. Turn the sandwiches with a spatula, and press to flatten them slightly. Cook until golden brown and the cheese is soft and creamy, about 2 minutes. Cut each sandwich into quarters and serve at once.

three-cheese pizza

Makes two 12-inch pizzas

Homemade pizza is a revelation, and it is perfect ski-weekend food because it can be as simple or as elaborate as you wish. You can make dough and sauce from scratch, or use shortcuts such as premade dough from the local market or pizzeria and store-bought tomato sauce. To make great homemade pizza it helps to have the proper equipment, like a pizza stone and paddle, but sturdy baking sheets and a super-hot oven will suffice.

PIZZA DOUGH:

1 cup warm water

1 package active dry yeast

3 tablespoons olive oil,
   plus more for brushing

Kosher salt

3 cups unbleached all-purpose flour

TOMATO SAUCE:

1½ tablespoons olive oil

4 cloves garlic, thinly sliced

1 can (28 ounces) crushed tomatoes
   with their juices

Kosher salt and freshly ground black pepper

¼ cup chopped fresh basil leaves

PIZZA:

Yellow cornmeal, for dusting

2 cups (½ pound) grated mozzarella cheese

1 cup (¼ pound) grated fontina cheese

½ cup freshly grated Parmesan cheese

¼ cup chopped fresh basil

1. To prepare the pizza dough, pour the water into a large mixing bowl. Sprinkle the yeast over it and let dissolve for 5 minutes. Whisk in the oil and a pinch of salt. Using a wooden spoon, mix in the flour, ½ cup at a time, to make a soft and sticky dough. Turn the dough out onto a floured surface and knead until smooth, about 8 minutes.

2. Brush another large mixing bowl with additional oil. Divide the dough into 2 balls and transfer to the bowl. Cover with a towel and let rise in a warm place until doubled, about 2½ hours. *continued*

3. To prepare the tomato sauce, heat the oil over medium heat in a large nonreactive saucepan and sauté the garlic until golden, about 2 minutes. Do not let the garlic burn.

4. Add the tomatoes and their juices and salt and pepper to taste to the saucepan and simmer, uncovered, until the sauce is thickened, about 30 minutes. Add the basil and cook a few minutes more. Taste and adjust the seasonings, if necessary.

5. Preheat the oven to 450°F and put a pizza stone or heavy-bottomed baking sheet in it to heat.

6. Flatten the dough on a surface dusted with cornmeal. Using a rolling pin, roll out the dough to roughly 12 inches in diameter, about ¼ inch thick. Dust a pizza paddle or baking sheet with cornmeal and transfer the pizza dough onto it. Working very quickly, spoon half the sauce over the dough and spread evenly. Sprinkle half the cheeses evenly over the sauce, and top with half of the basil. Slide the pizza onto the pizza stone or baking sheet and bake until the dough is golden brown and the cheese is bubbly and golden, 15 to 20 minutes. Repeat for the other pizza.

some other great pizza combinations

These are just suggestions for preparations, so quantities of butter and oil for slow-cooking or sautéing are general.

caramelized red onions & gorgonzola cheese
Slowly cook 4 thinly sliced red onions in butter and olive oil for about an hour. Spread the dough with the onions and sprinkle with about ¼ pound of Gorgonzola cheese and freshly ground black pepper.

caramelized onions, goat cheese, & pancetta
Slowly cook 4 thinly sliced onions in butter and olive oil for about an hour. Crumble about ¼ pound of softened goat cheese into the onions. Spread this mixture over the pizza dough and top with slices of pancetta.

red & yellow bell peppers with mozzarella cheese & sausage
Slowly cook a mixture of 3 thinly sliced bell peppers, 3 thinly sliced onions, 2 thinly sliced garlic cloves, and salt and pepper in butter and olive oil for about an hour. Sprinkle the dough with about ¼ pound of mozzarella cheese and top with the pepper mixture. Sauté and drain about ¼ pound of sausage meat and sprinkle over the pizza.

tomato sauce, mushrooms, & taleggio cheese
Sauté about 1 cup each fresh and wild mushrooms in butter and olive oil until browned and softened. Spread the dough with tomato sauce and the cooked mushrooms. Sprinkle with about ¼ pound of Taleggio cheese and freshly ground black pepper.

chapter 3

warm & wonderful soups

is there anything better than the aroma of homemade soup warming on the stove after coming inside from a chilly winter's day? Few dishes give us a greater sense of well-being than good, homemade soup. It can be a thick and hearty meal in itself for a winter lunch or dinner, or it may be served as a delicious starter for a dinner party. And since most soups taste better the day after they're made, making them can be nicely timed to fit into any busy person's schedule—whether cooking during the week or entertaining friends and family on the weekend.

white bean & sausage minestrone

serves 6 to 8

Here is a very hearty version of minestrone, the quintessential Italian vegetable and bean soup—
a perfect lunch or dinner to drive away the chill after a day of wintry activities.

½ cup dried white beans, soaked
overnight and drained

1 quart water

3 tablespoons olive oil

2 fennel bulbs, trimmed
and coarsely chopped

2 cups sliced leeks
(white and green parts)

2 carrots, finely chopped

3 cloves garlic, thinly sliced

4 cups chicken broth

1 can (28 ounces) tomatoes, coarsely chopped,
with their juices

Kosher salt and freshly ground pepper

½ pound kale, large stems discarded,
leaves finely chopped

¼ cup chopped basil leaves

1 cup cooked macaroni

½ to ¾ pound chicken sausage links

Freshly grated Parmesan cheese, for serving

1. Put the beans and water in a medium saucepan and bring to a boil. Reduce the heat to
   low, cover, and simmer until just tender, 25 to 30 minutes. Drain, and set aside.

2. Meanwhile, heat the olive oil in a large heavy soup pot or Dutch oven. Add the fennel, leeks,
   carrots, and garlic and cook, stirring, for 5 minutes. Add the broth, tomatoes and their juices,
   and salt and pepper to taste. Bring to a boil and simmer gently for 20 minutes. (The soup may
   be cooked up to this point and refrigerated until just before serving.)

3. About 15 minutes before serving, add the beans, kale, basil, and macaroni and cook over very
   low heat, stirring occasionally.

4. Meanwhile, cook the sausages in a broiler or sauté in a skillet until lightly browned. Set aside
   and drain. When cool enough to handle, cut into ¼-inch rounds.

5. Ladle the soup into bowls, scatter the sausage over each serving, and serve with Parmesan.

wild mushroom, chicken, & orzo soup

serves 6 to 8

This flavorful soup, made with porcini, cremini, and shiitake mushrooms, is a fantastic bowl of comfort food. Try it—you'll love it, especially since it's as easy as it is enjoyable, and gives your guests the feeling you must have been cooking all day to make something so restorative.

1½ ounces dried porcini mushrooms

3 tablespoons olive oil

1 onion, diced

3 cloves garlic, thinly sliced

3 stalks celery, diced

3 carrots, peeled and diced

4 cups chicken broth

2 cups water

½ cup chopped cremini mushrooms

½ cup chopped shiitake mushrooms

1 whole boneless, skinless chicken breast (about 1 pound), sliced into ½-inch strips

½ teaspoon cayenne pepper

½ teaspoon celery seed

Kosher salt and freshly ground black pepper

1 cup cooked orzo

2 teaspoons balsamic vinegar

½ cup chopped fresh flat-leaf parsley

1. In a small bowl, cover the porcini with 1½ cups boiling water and let sit for 30 minutes. Strain through a fine sieve and reserve the liquid. Finely chop the porcini and set aside.

2. In a large soup pot, heat 2 tablespoons of the olive oil over medium heat. Cook the onion and garlic until softened, about 5 minutes. Add the celery and carrots and cook 5 minutes. Add the broth and water and bring to a boil. Reduce the heat and simmer 20 minutes.

3. Meanwhile, heat the remaining 1 tablespoon of olive oil in a skillet and sauté the cremini and shiitake mushrooms until browned, about 5 minutes. Set aside.

4. Add 1 cup of the porcini liquid, the chicken, cayenne pepper, celery seed, and salt and pepper to taste to the soup and simmer for 10 minutes.

5. Add the mushrooms and porcini, orzo, vinegar, and parsley and simmer for 5 minutes. Taste and adjust the seasonings and serve at once.

green & yellow split pea soup

serves 6 to 8

This hearty, stick-to-your-ribs soup, made with both green and yellow split peas, is very tasty, and because dried peas are high in protein and dietary fiber and low in fat, it is also very good for you. If you want to go completely vegetarian with this one, use vegetable broth instead of chicken broth. Either way, it is excellent.

2 tablespoons olive oil
1 large onion, diced
3 carrots, peeled and diced
3 celery stalks, trimmed and diced
1½ cups dried green split peas
1½ cups dried yellow split peas
4 cups chicken or vegetable broth

4 cups water
1 teaspoon finely chopped fresh rosemary
1 teaspoon finely chopped fresh thyme
1 teaspoon celery seed
Kosher salt and freshly ground black pepper
½ cup chopped fresh parsley, for garnish

1. Heat the oil in a large soup pot or Dutch oven. Add the onion, carrots, and celery and cook over medium heat until tender, 8 to 10 minutes.
2. Add the peas, broth, and water and bring to a boil. Reduce the heat and simmer, uncovered, stirring occasionally, for ½ hour. Add the rosemary, thyme, celery seed, and salt and pepper to taste and simmer, stirring occasionally, until the peas are tender, about 45 minutes. Remove from the heat and let cool.
3. When cool enough to handle, transfer one half of the soup to a food processor and blend until very smooth. Return to the soup pot and stir well to blend. Heat the soup over medium heat until warmed through. Taste and adjust the seasonings, if necessary.
4. Ladle the soup into bowls, garnish with parsley, and serve at once.

corn chowder

serves 6

Delicate and mellow but substantial and satisfying, a bowl of steaming corn chowder is lovely to serve as a starter or a light main course for a wintry night's meal.

3 slices thick bacon

1½ cups diced onion

2 carrots, peeled and finely diced

1 celery stalk, finely diced

1 medium red bell pepper, seeded, deveined, and finely diced

4 medium Yukon Gold potatoes, peeled and cut into ¼-inch dice

4 cups chicken broth

1 cup water

1 teaspoon chopped fresh thyme

3 cups fresh corn (4 or 5 ears)

1½ cups whole milk

1 cup heavy cream

Pinch of red pepper flakes

Kosher salt and freshly ground black pepper

½ cup chopped fresh cherry or plum tomatoes, for garnish

½ cup chopped fresh flat-leaf parsley, for garnish

1. In a large soup pot, cook the bacon until crisp, and drain on paper towels. Add the onion, carrots, celery, and bell pepper to the bacon fat and cook, stirring, until softened, 8 to 10 minutes.

2. Add the potatoes, broth, water, and thyme and simmer, partially covered, until the potatoes are just tender, about 15 minutes. Add the corn, milk, cream, and red pepper flakes and simmer, uncovered, until warmed through, about 10 minutes. Season to taste with salt and pepper.

3. To serve, ladle the soup into shallow bowls. Crumble the bacon and sprinkle it over the soup. Garnish with tomatoes and parsley and serve at once.

mushroom barley soup

serves 6

A mix of fresh mushrooms and porcini broth adds a deep and woodsy richness to this take on classic mushroom barley soup. Nothing tastes better on a cold winter afternoon, and mushrooms are full of antioxidants and nutrients that can help strengthen immune systems, so they're especially great to use in cold-weather meals.

½ cup dried porcini

2 tablespoons olive oil

1 medium onion, diced

2 stalks celery, diced

1 medium carrot, diced

½ pound cremini mushrooms, trimmed and coarsely chopped (see Note)

¼ pound shiitake mushrooms, trimmed and coarsely chopped

½ cup pearl barley

6 cups chicken broth

2 tablespoons dry sherry

½ teaspoon celery seed

Kosher salt and freshly ground black pepper

½ cup chopped fresh flat-leaf parsley, for garnish

1. In a small bowl, cover the porcini with 1½ cups boiling water and let sit for 30 minutes. Strain through a fine sieve and reserve the liquid. Finely chop the porcini and set aside.

2. Heat the oil in a soup pot. Sauté the onion, celery, and carrot over medium heat until softened. Add the mushrooms and sauté, stirring often, for about 8 minutes, until they begin to release their liquid.

3. Raise the heat and add the barley, and sauté until it begins to color. Add the broth and sherry. Add the porcini and reserved liquid. Add the celery seed and salt and pepper to taste, bring to a boil, reduce the heat, and simmer, uncovered, for about 45 minutes, until the barley is tender. Taste and adjust the seasonings, if necessary. Garnish each serving with fresh parsley and serve at once.

Note: If cremini mushrooms are not available, you may substitute white mushrooms.

roasted acorn squash soup

serves 6 to 8

When a simple acorn squash is roasted with carrots and onions, it can be transformed into a refined and fragrant, creamy soup that gets a cold-weather dinner off to a delicious start.

3 acorn squash, seeded and halved

4 carrots, cut crosswise
   into ½-inch lengths

1 onion, quartered

1 tablespoon unsalted butter

1 tablespoon light brown sugar

4 cups chicken broth

Kosher salt and freshly ground black pepper

2 cups water

½ teaspoon ground ginger

Pinch of cayenne pepper

1 cup whole milk

2 tablespoons snipped fresh chives, for garnish

1. Preheat the oven to 375°F.
2. Put the squash halves, cut side up, in a large roasting pan and distribute the carrots and onion around them. Dot the vegetables with butter and sprinkle with brown sugar. Pour 1 cup of the broth over the vegetables and season to taste with salt and pepper. Cover with aluminum foil and bake for about 1 hour or until the squash is tender.
3. Let the squash cool in the pan until cool enough to handle. Scoop the squash flesh from the skins and transfer to a stockpot; discard the skins. Add the carrots, onion, any pan juices, the water, and the remaining 3 cups of broth. Bring to a boil over high heat, reduce the heat to medium, stir in the ginger, and cayenne pepper, and simmer, uncovered, for about 20 minutes.
4. Transfer the soup to a food processor or blender and puree until smooth. This will have to be done in batches. Return it to the pot. (At this point, the soup may be refrigerated, covered, for 2 or 3 days or frozen for up to a month.)
5. Bring the soup to a gentle boil over medium heat. Add the milk, stir well, season to taste with salt and pepper, and cook until piping hot. Ladle into soup bowls and garnish with chives.

chili three ways

Few dishes are as comfortingly familiar in cold weather as chili. Here is a recipe for a chili base that can be made either well in advance or on the day you're serving it. You can then make chili in many ways: with beef and beans (page 63); with turkey and beans (page 62); or as a vegetarian dish made with vegetable broth instead of chicken broth and a variety of beans (page 62). The chili base is an excellent freezer staple to have on hand all winter.

3 tablespoons olive oil

2 onions, finely diced

4 scallions (white and green parts), trimmed and minced

3 cloves garlic, thinly sliced

2 jalapeño peppers, seeded and finely diced

2 tablespoons ground cumin

2 tablespoons chili powder

1 tablespoon ground coriander

1 tablespoon paprika

Pinch of red pepper flakes

2 cans (28 ounces each) plum tomatoes, coarsely chopped, with their juices

1 bottle (12 ounces) dark beer

1 cup chicken or vegetable broth

Kosher salt and freshly ground black pepper

1. Heat the oil in a large soup pot or Dutch oven. Add the onions, scallions, and garlic and sauté over medium heat, stirring occasionally, until soft and translucent, about 10 minutes. Stir in the jalapeños and cook 5 minutes more.

2. Put the cumin, chili powder, coriander, paprika, and red pepper flakes in a dry skillet and toast them over medium-high heat, stirring constantly with a wooden spoon and being careful not to burn them, 2 to 3 minutes. Let cool, then add it to the onions and cook 5 minutes more.

3. Add the tomatoes and their juices, beer, broth, and salt and pepper to taste and bring to a boil, then turn down the heat and simmer over medium heat for about 30 minutes. (The base may be prepared up to this point and will keep in the refrigerator for up to 3 days or in the freezer for up to 1 month. If stored, bring to room temperature before final cooking.)

turkey & bean chili

serves 8

2 pounds ground turkey
I can (15.5 ounces) kidney beans, drained and rinsed
I can (15.5 ounces) black beans, drained and rinsed
Kosher salt and freshly ground black pepper

1. About ½ hour before serving, bring the chili base to a low simmer.
2. Sauté the turkey in a skillet over medium-high heat. Crumble the meat and cook just until it is no longer pink. Drain the fat and add the meat to the chili base and mix well.
3. Add the beans to the chili and season to taste with salt and pepper. If the mixture seems too thick, thin with water or more beer. Simmer the chili over low heat for 30 minutes. Serve warm with accompaniments.

vegetarian chili

serves 8

I can (15.5 ounces) kidney beans, drained and rinsed
I can (15.5 ounces) black beans, drained and rinsed
I can (15.5 ounces) pinto beans, drained and rinsed
Kosher salt and freshly ground black pepper

1. About ½ hour before serving, bring the chili base to a low simmer.
2. Add the beans to the chili and season to taste with salt and pepper. If the mixture seems too thick, thin with water or more beer. Simmer the chili over low heat for 30 minutes. Serve warm with accompaniments.

beef & bean chili

serves 8

1 tablespoon olive oil

2 pounds ground sirloin or chuck

¼ cup tomato paste

1 can (15.5 ounces) kidney beans, drained and rinsed

1 can (15.5 ounces) black beans, drained and rinsed

Pinch of ground cinnamon

Kosher salt and freshly ground black pepper

1. About ½ hour before serving, bring the chili base to a low simmer.
2. Heat the olive oil in a large skillet. Add the beef and sauté over medium-high heat. Crumble the meat and cook just until it is no longer pink. Drain the fat. Add the tomato paste and cook, stirring, about 2 minutes. Add to the chili base and mix well.
3. Add the beans to the chili and season to taste with the cinnamon and the salt and pepper. If the mixture seems too thick, thin with water or more beer. Simmer the chili over low heat for 30 minutes. Serve warm with accompaniments.

accompaniments for chili

grated cheddar cheese	chopped red, yellow, & green bell peppers
sour cream	chopped jalapeños or other chiles
diced tomatoes	chopped lettuce
chopped red onions	chopped avocados or guacamole
chopped scallions	chopped fresh cilantro, parsley, & chives

chapter 4

main dishes

crisp weather makes us crave robust and restorative food such as short ribs, briskets, stews, and pastas. It's no wonder—we need those substantial meals to keep our energy up throughout the cold seasons. This chapter is full of uncomplicated and satisfying recipes that will fill your kitchen with the inviting aromas of your favorite ski-season dishes, and will keep you, your family, and your guests warm and happy all winter.

italian-style chicken stew

serves 4 to 6

This dish is based on the traditional Italian chicken *alla cacciatore* (hunter-style chicken), with an addition of fresh white and shiitake mushrooms to add depth and richness.

One 3½-pound chicken, cut into 10 pieces

Kosher salt and freshly ground black pepper

2 tablespoons olive oil

1 medium onion, thinly sliced

1 cup thinly sliced white mushrooms

1 cup thinly sliced shiitake mushrooms

2 cloves garlic, thinly sliced

1 cup dry white wine

2 tablespoons Marsala wine

1 can (15 ounces) peeled plum tomatoes, coarsely chopped, with their juices

½ cup chicken broth

1 teaspoon minced fresh thyme leaves

¼ cup chopped fresh flat-leaf parsley, for garnish

1. Pat the chicken dry and season to taste with salt and pepper. In a large skillet with a lid, heat the oil over medium-high heat. Add the chicken (in batches if necessary) and cook, turning, until browned, about 7 minutes. Transfer to a plate.

2. Add the onion to the pan and cook, stirring occasionally, for 3 minutes. Add the white and shiitake mushrooms and the garlic and cook, stirring until the mushrooms are softened, about 5 minutes.

3. Pour in the white wine and Marsala and bring to a boil, scraping up any browned bits from the bottom of the pan. Add the tomatoes and their juices, broth, and thyme. Bring to a boil again and return the chicken to the pan along with its accumulated juices.

4. Reduce the heat and simmer, partially covered, turning the chicken pieces occasionally, for 40 to 45 minutes. The chicken should be very tender and the sauce slightly reduced and thickened. Season to taste with more salt and pepper, if necessary. Garnish with parsley and serve.

cider-braised chicken & vegetables

serves 4 to 6

This earthy dish of chicken simmered in apple cider and white wine makes a wonderful meal-in-a-bowl to serve for an intimate dinner.

8 chicken thighs
  (about 2½ pounds)
Kosher salt and freshly ground
  black pepper
2 tablespoons unsalted butter
1 tablespoon olive oil
2 shallots, minced
1½ cups apple cider
1 cup dry white wine
1 cup chicken broth

1 teaspoon cider vinegar
2 medium carrots, peeled and cut on the diagonal
2 medium parsnips, peeled and
  cut on the diagonal
2 medium red potatoes, scrubbed and
  cut into 1-inch pieces
1 teaspoon Dijon mustard
1 tablespoon heavy cream
1 tablespoon fresh lemon juice
½ cup chopped fresh flat-leaf parsley, for garnish

1. Pat the chicken dry and season to taste with salt and pepper. In a large skillet, melt the butter and oil over medium heat. Add the chicken and sauté, turning, until golden, about 5 to 7 minutes. Transfer the chicken to a plate. Pour off all but 1 tablespoon oil from the pan.

2. Add the shallots to the pan and cook over medium heat until softened and fragrant, about 1 minute. Pour in the cider and wine and bring to a boil, scraping up all the browned bits from the bottom of the pan. Reduce the heat and simmer for 5 minutes.

3. Add the broth, vinegar, and additional salt and pepper to taste. Return the chicken to the pan along with any juices that have accumulated on the plate. Add the carrots, parsnips and potatoes. Bring to a boil and simmer over low heat until tender, 25 to 30 minutes.

4. Transfer the chicken and vegetables to a serving dish with a slotted spoon. Bring the sauce to a simmer, add the mustard and cream, and whisk until well combined. Add the lemon juice and whisk again. Pour the sauce over the chicken, garnish with parsley, and serve at once.

turkey & vegetable meat loaf

serves 6 to 8

This light and moist version of meat loaf is made more distinctive with yogurt and sautéed vegetables, plus a kick of chili to heat it up for wintertime. It might be a good idea to double the recipe and make two loaves, so you'll have leftovers to use for tasty sandwiches.

1 tablespoon olive oil,
   plus more for coating pan

¾ cup finely chopped onion

1 clove garlic, finely minced

½ cup finely chopped red or yellow
   bell pepper

½ cup finely chopped celery

2 pounds ground turkey

¼ cup thinly sliced scallions

½ cup cooked fresh or frozen corn kernels

1 cup bread crumbs

½ cup plain yogurt

1 egg, lightly beaten

½ cup bottled chili sauce

1 teaspoon dried thyme

½ teaspoon celery seed

Kosher salt and freshly ground black pepper

1. Preheat the oven to 350°F. Lightly coat a 5-by-9-inch loaf pan with olive oil.

2. Heat 1 tablespoon of olive oil in a large skillet. Cook the onion, garlic, bell pepper, and celery over medium-high heat until softened, about 7 minutes. Remove from the heat and let cool.

3. Put the turkey, scallions, corn, bread crumbs, and yogurt in a large bowl. Add the sautéed vegetables and gently mix the ingredients together with your hands. Add the egg, ¼ cup of the chili sauce, the thyme, celery seed, and salt and pepper to taste, and mix again.

4. Transfer the mixture and pack into the prepared pan. Bake for 30 minutes. Spread the remaining ¼ cup of the chili sauce over the loaf and bake for an additional 30 minutes. Let stand for about 10 minutes before slicing and serving.

duck breasts with red wine, oranges, & olives

serves 4 to 6

Duck breasts, though quite elegant, are easy to prepare and ideal for entertaining because once they are seared, they will keep well in a barely warm oven. This rich winter dish is fabulous served with wild rice and haricots verts.

2 tablespoons light soy sauce	2 shallots, minced
I teaspoon chili paste	I teaspoon fresh thyme leaves
2 teaspoons five-spice powder	I cup dry red wine
Freshly ground black pepper	½ cup orange pieces
2 duck breasts, about I pound each	¼ cup black olives, pitted and halved
2 tablespoons unsalted butter	

1. In a small bowl, whisk together the soy sauce, chili paste, five-spice powder, and pepper to taste. Score the fat side of the duck breasts in a criss-cross pattern. Rub the breasts on both sides with the marinade. Set aside for 2 hours.
2. Preheat the oven to 250°F.
3. In a cast-iron skillet, sear the duck breasts over high heat until well browned on all sides. Transfer to a baking dish and bake for 45 minutes.
4. Melt I tablespoon of the butter in a skillet, add the shallots, and cook until softened. Stir in the thyme and half the wine. Cook until the wine reduces by one-third. Remove from the heat.
5. A few minutes before serving, bring the sauce to a simmer. Stir in the remaining butter and wine and simmer for 5 minutes, stirring occasionally. Add the oranges and olives and simmer for 5 more minutes.
6. To serve, cut the duck on the bias into thin slices and arrange on a serving platter. Spoon the sauce over the duck and serve at once.

beef brisket
with creamy horseradish sauce

serves 6 to 8

Beef brisket is another cold-weather comfort food that nearly everyone loves. Here it gets its great taste from slow cooking a day or two before serving, so plan accordingly. Lively horseradish sauce is an excellent accompaniment to the mellow beef.

2 tablespoons olive oil

3 medium onions, coarsely chopped

3 cloves garlic, thinly sliced

1 first-cut brisket (3 to 4 pounds)

Kosher salt and freshly ground
    black pepper

1 can (14½ to 16 ounces) whole
    plum tomatoes, coarsely chopped,
    with their juices

1½ cups dry white wine

2 stalks celery, chopped

1 bay leaf

1 teaspoon chopped fresh rosemary leaves

1 teaspoon chopped fresh oregano

3 carrots, peeled and cut into ½-inch slices

½ cup chopped fresh parsley

HORSERADISH SAUCE:

½ cup heavy (whipping) cream

½ cup mayonnaise

½ cup prepared horseradish

1 tablespoon Dijon mustard

Pinch of sugar

Kosher salt and freshly ground black pepper

1. Preheat the oven to 350°F.
2. Heat 1 tablespoon of the oil in a large casserole or Dutch oven over medium heat. Add the onions and garlic and cook, stirring, until softened and golden, about 10 minutes. Remove from the heat.

3. Season the brisket generously with salt and pepper. In a large skillet, heat the remaining 1 tablespoon of oil over high heat. Add the brisket and cook, turning, until browned, about 4 minutes per side. Put the brisket in the casserole, fat side up, on top of the onions. Add the tomatoes and their juices, wine, celery, bay leaf, rosemary, and oregano.

4. Cover the casserole and bake 2½ hours, basting with the pan juices and turning the meat occasionally. Add the carrots and parsley and continue baking, uncovered, until the carrots are tender, about 30 minutes. Let the brisket cool in the pan, then cover and refrigerate. (The brisket will keep in the refrigerator for up to 2 days.)

5. About 1 hour before serving, preheat the oven to 350°F. Transfer the brisket to a shallow roasting pan or baking dish and spoon the juices and vegetables on top. Cover tightly with foil and bake until heated through, about 45 minutes.

6. Meanwhile, prepare the horseradish sauce. Whip the heavy cream in a bowl until it forms soft peaks. In another bowl, combine the mayonnaise, horseradish, and mustard. Add the sugar and salt and pepper to taste and stir well. Fold the horseradish mixture into the whipped cream until blended. The sauce will keep, covered, in the refrigerator for 3 hours.

7. Transfer the brisket to a cutting board and slice across the grain into ¼-inch slices. Arrange the meat and vegetables on a platter, drizzle with the juices, and serve with the horseradish sauce on the side.

red wine–braised short ribs

serves 6

The rich meaty taste of short ribs makes them a favorite winter dish, and the smell of them slow-simmering on the stovetop infuses the whole house. I love to serve them with roasted potatoes or Mashed Potatoes with Shallots and Garlic (page 106).

1 bottle of dry red wine

4 to 5 pounds short ribs

Kosher salt and freshly ground
   black pepper

12 shallots or pearl onions,
   peeled and trimmed

6 cloves garlic, halved

2 tablespoons Dijon mustard

6 canned plum tomatoes, coarsely chopped,
   with their juices

1 tablespoon chopped fresh thyme

½ cup chopped fresh parsley, for garnish

1. Put the wine in a heavy-bottomed saucepan and boil until it is reduced by half. Set aside.
2. Meanwhile, season the short ribs generously with salt and pepper. Heat a large soup pot or Dutch oven and brown the ribs over medium-high heat on all sides. This will have to be done in batches. Transfer the ribs to a bowl.
3. Reduce the heat and brown the shallots or onions and garlic in the remaining fat, stirring often, until softened, about 5 minutes. Transfer to another bowl.
4. Pour the wine into the pot, add the mustard, and whisk until well combined. Add the ribs and simmer, covered, for 1 hour, turning the ribs occasionally. Stir in the shallots or onions, garlic, tomatoes and their juices, and thyme and continue to simmer, covered, until the meat is very tender, about 1 hour more.
5. Transfer the ribs and shallots or onions to a platter or large shallow bowl. Skim off any fat from the sauce and pour over the ribs. Garnish with parsley and serve.

slow-cooked beef & vegetable stew

serves 6 to 8

With this ultra-simple recipe, you can be out all day in the snow but still come back to a delicious warm stew fresh from the oven. It's a perfect thing to cook on ski weekends, and at home during the busy work week as well.

2 pounds beef, round or chuck,
  cut into 1-inch cubes

4 small red potatoes,
  cut into 1½-inch cubes

3 medium carrots, peeled
  and cut into 1-inch pieces

3 medium parsnips, peeled
  and cut into 1-inch pieces

6 large shallots, peeled and
  left whole

1 cup sliced white or cremini mushrooms

½ cup thinly sliced shiitake mushrooms

Kosher salt and freshly ground black pepper

1 cup canned plum tomatoes, coarsely chopped,
  with their juices

1½ cups beef or chicken broth

1½ cups dry red wine, such as Côtes du Rhône

1. Preheat the oven to 200°F.
2. Put the beef, potatoes, carrots, parsnips, shallots, and mushrooms in a large Dutch oven. Season generously with the salt and pepper. Add the tomatoes and their juices, broth, and wine and stir to mix well.
3. Put in the oven and cook at least 6 to 8 hours. The meat should be fork-tender. Serve at once.

beef & green chili tacos

serves 8 to 10

Tacos are great to serve to a crowd of hungry skiers. They're fast, fresh, and satisfying after an active day. The filling may be prepared well ahead of time, and your guests can customize their tacos with an array of readily available ingredients.

2 tablespoons corn oil

2 pounds ground beef

2 cups finely diced red onion

2 cloves garlic, thinly sliced

1 tablespoon finely diced
 jalapeño pepper

2 tablespoons chili powder

1 tablespoon ground cumin

1 tablespoon hot paprika

3 tablespoons canned green chiles

2 cups puréed plum tomatoes

1 cup dark beer

Kosher salt and freshly ground black pepper

About 20 hard taco shells

Grated cheddar cheese, sour cream, diced tomatoes, chopped red onions, chopped jalapeños or other chiles, chopped scallions, chopped bell peppers, chopped lettuce, diced avocados or guacamole, chopped fresh cilantro, parsley, and chives, for serving

1. Heat 1 tablespoon of the oil in a large skillet over medium-high heat. Add the beef and sauté over medium-high heat. Crumble the meat and cook just until it is no longer pink. Transfer the meat to a strainer and strain well.

2. Wipe out the skillet and add the remaining 1 tablespoon of oil. Add the onion and garlic and sauté for 2 minutes. Add the jalapeño pepper and sauté for 1 minute. Add the chili powder, cumin, and paprika and cook, stirring, until the spices are well blended into the onion mixture, about 2 minutes. Add the drained meat, chiles, tomatoes, beer, and salt and pepper to taste. Simmer for 20 to 25 minutes or until the sauce has thickened. (The taco filling may be prepared up to this point and will keep in the refrigerator for up to 3 days or in the freezer for up to 1 month. Bring to room temperature before final cooking.)

3. Serve warm with accompaniments.

asian-style pan-roasted spare ribs

serves 6

When we think of spare ribs, we usually think of grilling. But meaty country-style spare ribs taste fabulous when oven-roasted and braised in red wine and soy sauce, with orange zest and Asian spices to add a little zing. This dish pairs especially well with Stir-Fried Coleslaw (page 103), and together they bring the warmth of a summer barbecue to your ski vacation.

3½ to 4 pounds pork spare ribs
  (country-style)
Kosher salt and freshly ground
  black pepper
6 large garlic cloves,
  peeled and halved
⅓ cup olive oil
½ cup chicken broth

1½ cups dry red wine
⅓ cup light soy sauce
1 tablespoon orange zest
1 tablespoon honey
1 teaspoon Thai chili paste
1 tablespoon five-spice powder
1 tablespoon minced fresh ginger

1. Preheat the oven to 425°F.
2. Cut the spare ribs between the bones into single ribs. Pat them dry and season well with salt and pepper.
3. Put the ribs and the garlic in a large roasting pan, pour the oil over them, and toss well to coat. Pour in the broth and roast, turning occasionally, until the ribs are lightly browned, about 30 minutes. Remove from the oven and pour off any remaining liquid from the pan.
4. Meanwhile, stir the wine, soy sauce, orange zest, honey, chili paste, five-spice powder, and ginger together until well combined.
5. Pour the wine mixture over the ribs and turn to coat them well. Continue baking, turning occasionally, until the ribs are browned, about 30 minutes. Serve the ribs and sauce at once.

baked ham
with maple-ginger glaze

serves 10 to 12

Perfectly baked ham—sweet and deeply browned on the outside and tender and juicy on the inside—is a perfect centerpiece for a big winter celebration dinner. The ginger and maple-syrup glaze for this ham is sweet, simple, and delicious.

One 5- to 6-pound cooked half ham, bone in, excess fat trimmed

MAPLE-GINGER GLAZE:

2 tablespoons grated fresh ginger

¼ cup maple syrup

1. Preheat the oven to 325°F. Line a shallow roasting pan with aluminum foil and set a roasting rack in the pan.
2. Put the ham, fat side up, on the rack and bake for 1½ to 2 hours.
3. To make the glaze, whisk the ginger and maple syrup together until well blended. About 30 minutes before the ham is done, brush it all over with the glaze. Continue baking, basting the ham once or twice. Let the ham stand for 10 to 15 minutes before carving and serving.

oven-braised pork roast

serves 6

This savory pork dish is excellent to make for winter dinner parties. The roast is first browned and then gently braised in the oven with onions, garlic, and white wine. Sliced and served with a sauce made with the braising juices and mustard, it tastes every bit as good as it looks.

One 3½ to 4 pound boneless
   pork loin

Kosher salt and freshly ground
   black pepper

2 tablespoons corn, canola,
   or safflower oil

2 onions, coarsely chopped

6 large garlic cloves, peeled and halved

1 teaspoon chopped fresh rosemary

1 teaspoon chopped fresh thyme

½ cup dry white wine

1 teaspoon Dijon mustard

¼ cup chopped fresh parsley

1. Preheat the oven to 350°F. Pat the meat dry and season generously on all sides with salt and pepper.
2. In a large soup pot or Dutch oven with a lid, heat the oil over medium heat. Add the meat and brown, turning on all sides, about 10 minutes. Remove the meat and set aside.
3. Put the onions and garlic in the pot and cook until softened, scraping up any browned bits, about 7 minutes. Add the rosemary and thyme and cook, stirring, for 1 minute. Add the wine and bring to a simmer.
4. Return the meat to the pot, cover, and put it in the oven. Cook for 1 hour and 10 minutes, basting the roast every 20 minutes, until a meat thermometer inserted in the center registers 160°F. Remove the meat to a cutting board and let sit for 5 minutes.
5. Meanwhile, bring the liquid in the pot to a low boil. Add the mustard and whisk until thickened. Add the parsley and whisk again.
6. Slice the roast into ½-inch slices and arrange on a platter. Spoon the sauce over the meat and serve at once.

braised lentils & sausage

serves 6

This cozy dish is winter comfort food at its best, and is simple and adaptable. It can be made with easy-to-find ingredients from the market, such as packaged kielbasa, French garlic sausage, or any other cooked sausage, in any combination.

2 tablespoons olive oil

1 onion, diced

2 garlic cloves, thinly sliced

2 ribs celery, diced

2 carrots, peeled and diced

1 pound lentils

3 tablespoons chopped fresh
flat-leaf parsley

1 teaspoon chopped fresh thyme

2 cups chicken, beef, or vegetable broth

1½ pounds fully cooked sausage,
such as kielbasa or French garlic sausage,
sliced into 1-inch rounds

1 cup water

Kosher salt and freshly ground black pepper

Dijon mustard, for serving

1. Heat the oil over medium heat in a large heavy-bottomed saucepan or Dutch oven. Add the onion, garlic, celery, and carrots and cook, stirring, until softened, about 10 minutes. Do not let the vegetables brown.

2. Add the lentils, 2 tablespoons of the parsley, the thyme, and broth and stir well to combine. Simmer the mixture, partially covered, stirring occasionally, for 15 minutes.

3. Add the sausage, water, and salt and pepper to taste and continue to cook, partially covered, stirring occasionally, until the lentils are tender, about 20 minutes. Taste and adjust the seasonings, if necessary. Transfer to a large bowl, garnish with the remaining 1 tablespoon of parsley, and serve with mustard on the side.

spicy lamb shanks

serves 6

Certain cuts of meat benefit deliciously from slow simmering, and lamb shanks are certainly among them. This soul-satisfying dish will sate your hunger on a long, cold winter night.

6 lamb shanks, ¾ to 1 pound each
Kosher salt and freshly ground
　　black pepper
1 tablespoon olive oil
1 onion, diced
3 garlic cloves, thinly sliced
3 ribs celery, diced
3 carrots, peeled and diced
1 cup dry white wine

1 can (28 ounces) plum tomatoes,
　　coarsely chopped, with their juices
2 cups chicken broth
1 teaspoon chili powder
½ teaspoon hot paprika
Pinch of cayenne pepper
1 teaspoon chopped fresh thyme
½ cup chopped fresh flat-leaf parsley, for garnish

1. Season the shanks generously with salt and pepper. Heat the oil in a large heavy-bottomed saucepan or Dutch oven. Add the lamb shanks and sear over medium heat until golden brown, about 5 minutes per side. Remove and set aside.

2. Put the onion, garlic, celery, and carrots in the pan and sauté until softened, about 10 minutes. Add the wine and cook for about 2 minutes, scraping the bottom of the pan with a wooden spoon to loosen any browned bits.

3. Add the tomatoes and their juices, broth, chili powder, paprika, cayenne pepper, and thyme. Return the shanks to the pan and bring to a boil. Reduce the heat and simmer, partially covered, over medium-low heat until the lamb is very tender, 2 to 2½ hours, stirring and turning the shanks occasionally. Season to taste with additional salt and pepper. Divide the shanks and sauce among 6 plates. Garnish with parsley and serve immediately.

lamb stew with white beans

serves 6

Hearty stews, which can and usually should be made ahead of time, are excellent cold-weather dishes, because of both their ease and their stick-to-the-ribs goodness. Serve this with nothing more than a salad of mixed greens and lots of crusty bread and red wine.

BEANS:

1 pound dried white beans, such as cannellini or great Northern

4 cups water

2 cups chicken broth

1 onion, peeled and halved

1 carrot, peeled and halved crosswise

6 sprigs fresh thyme

Kosher salt and freshly ground black pepper

STEW:

2½ pounds lamb stew meat, cut into 2-inch cubes

Kosher salt and freshly ground black pepper

3 tablespoons olive oil

2 cups chopped onions

1 tablespoon ground cumin

1 teaspoon paprika

3 carrots, peeled and diced

3 cups dry red wine

1 cup chicken broth

1 cup fresh or canned plum tomatoes, coarsely chopped, with their juices

½ cup chopped fresh parsley, for garnish

1. To prepare the beans, rinse them and put them in a large saucepan. Cover with cold water. Cover the pan and bring the water to a boil over high heat. Once boiling, remove the pan from the heat. Let rest, covered, for 40 minutes.

2. Drain the beans, discarding the cooking liquid. Add the 4 cups of water, the chicken broth, onion, carrot, thyme, and salt and pepper to taste. Bring to a simmer over medium heat and cook, uncovered, until the beans are tender, about 45 minutes. The beans should be firm-tender. Drain beans and discard the onion, carrot, and thyme. (The beans may be cooked in advance and then reheated.)

3. To prepare the stew, pat the lamb dry and sprinkle with salt and pepper. Heat 2 tablespoons of the oil over medium-high heat in a large soup pot or Dutch oven. When the oil is hot but not smoking, add the lamb in batches and brown on all sides, 5 to 7 minutes for each batch. Transfer the lamb with a slotted spoon to a bowl and wipe out the pot.

4. Heat the remaining 1 tablespoon of olive oil in the pot, add the onions, and sauté for 2 minutes. Add the cumin and paprika and mix well. Cook until the onions are softened, about 5 minutes. Add the carrots, wine, broth, and tomatoes and their juices, bring to a boil, reduce the heat, and simmer, partially covered, until the lamb is very tender, about 1½ hours. (The stew may be prepared up to this point and will keep in the refrigerator for up to 3 days or in the freezer for up to 1 month. Bring to room temperature before final cooking.)

5. To serve, divide the beans into soup bowls and spoon the stew over them. Garnish with parsley and serve at once.

baked penne with sausage & cheese

serves 6 to 8

This rich and creamy pasta dish is a wintertime staple in my house—adults, kids, and company alike can't seem to get enough of it. If you want to make a vegetarian version, simply omit the sausage when preparing the sauce.

2 tablespoons olive oil

1 onion, chopped

3 garlic cloves, thinly sliced

¾ pound pork, chicken, or turkey sausage, casings removed

1 can (28 ounces) plum tomatoes, coarsely chopped, with their juices

2 tablespoons chopped fresh basil

Pinch of red pepper flakes

Kosher salt and freshly ground black pepper

1 pound penne pasta

1 cup (¼ pound) ricotta cheese

1 cup (¼ pound) shredded mozzarella cheese

1 cup (¼ pound) shredded fontina cheese

½ cup freshly grated Parmesan cheese, plus more for serving (optional)

1. In a large soup pot or Dutch oven, heat the oil over medium heat. Add the onion and cook until softened, about 5 minutes. Add the garlic and cook for 1 minute. Add the sausage and cook until no longer pink, stirring and breaking it up, 6 to 8 minutes. Add the tomatoes and their juices, basil, red pepper flakes, and salt and pepper to taste and bring to a boil. Reduce the heat to medium-low and simmer, stirring occasionally, until thickened, 20 to 30 minutes.

2. Meanwhile, bring a large pot of salted water to a boil. Add the pasta and cook until al dente. Drain well and transfer to a large bowl. Add the sauce to the pasta, toss well, and let cool a bit.

3. Preheat the oven to 350°F. Lightly oil a 9½-by-14½- or 10-by-14-inch baking dish.

4. Toss the pasta and sauce with the ricotta, mozzarella, and fontina cheeses until well combined. Transfer to the prepared dish, spread evenly, and sprinkle with the Parmesan cheese.

5. Bake until the cheeses are melted and the tips of the pasta are golden brown, 30 to 35 minutes. Serve hot with additional Parmesan cheese, if desired.

creamy macaroni & cheese

serves 6

Who doesn't love mac and cheese? Lots of grated white and sharp cheddar cheeses give this classic dish a perfect hit of flavor that will please both the kids and the grown-ups at the table.

4 tablespoons unsalted butter,
plus more for the dish

2 cups diced onion

¼ cup unbleached all-purpose flour

3 cups warm whole milk

2 cups (½ pound) grated sharp
cheddar cheese

2 cups (½ pound) grated white cheddar cheese

2 tablespoons Dijon mustard

½ teaspoon Tabasco sauce or Louisiana hot sauce

½ teaspoon ground nutmeg

Kosher salt and freshly ground black pepper

1 pound elbow macaroni

4 tablespoons freshly grated Parmesan cheese

1. Preheat the oven to 350°F. Generously butter a 2-quart baking dish.
2. Melt the 4 tablespoons of butter in a large saucepan over medium heat. Cook the onion until soft but not browned. Add the flour and cook for 2 minutes, stirring constantly. Whisk in the milk until thoroughly blended. Cook, whisking constantly, until the mixture begins to thicken. Remove from the heat and stir in the cheddar cheese, mustard, hot sauce, nutmeg, and salt and pepper to taste.
3. Meanwhile, bring a large pot of salted water to a boil and cook the macaroni until al dente. Drain and return the macaroni to the pot. Add the cheese sauce and stir to blend well. Spoon the mixture into the prepared dish and sprinkle with the Parmesan cheese. (The dish may be prepared up to this point and refrigerated, covered, up to 8 hours ahead of time. Bring to room temperature before baking.)
4. Bake until the mixture is hot and bubbling, about 25 minutes. Remove and turn on the broiler. Brown the macaroni and cheese under the broiler until the top is nicely browned, about 3 minutes. Serve at once.

macaroni & cheese
with mushrooms & ham

serves 6 to 8

This version of macaroni & cheese is a fairly sophisticated one—full of creamy cheddar and Gruyère cheeses, mushrooms, and ham—so it's great for wintertime entertaining. Although it's very good with classic elbow macaroni, try making it with curly cavatappi.

5 tablespoons unsalted butter, plus more for the dish

¼ cup unbleached all-purpose flour

2 cups warm whole milk

2 cups (½ pound) grated sharp cheddar cheese

2 cups (½ pound) grated Gruyère cheese

½ teaspoon ground nutmeg

Pinch of cayenne pepper

Kosher salt and freshly ground black pepper

1½ cups diced onion

½ cup white or cremini mushrooms, stemmed and thinly sliced

½ cup shiitake mushrooms, stemmed and thinly sliced

½ pound cooked ham, cut into ¼-inch dice

1 cup heavy cream

1 pound elbow macaroni or cavatappi

4 tablespoons freshly grated Parmesan cheese

1. Preheat the oven to 350°F. Generously butter a 2-quart baking dish.

2. Melt 4 tablespoons of the butter in a large saucepan over medium heat. Add the flour and cook for 2 minutes, stirring constantly. Whisk in the milk until thoroughly blended. Cook, whisking constantly, until the mixture begins to thicken. Remove from the heat and stir in the cheddar and Gruyère cheeses, nutmeg, cayenne pepper, and salt and pepper to taste.

3. Melt the remaining 1 tablespoon of butter in a skillet and add the onion and mushrooms. Cook, stirring, until softened. Add the ham and cook, stirring, about 1 minute. Stir into the cheese sauce. Stir the cream into the sauce and stir to blend well. *continued*

4. Meanwhile, bring a large pot of salted water to a boil and cook the macaroni until al dente. Drain and return the macaroni to the pot. Add the cheese sauce and stir to blend well. Spoon the mixture into the prepared dish and sprinkle with the Parmesan cheese. (The dish may be prepared up to this point and refrigerated, covered, up to 8 hours ahead of time. Bring to room temperature before baking.)

5. Bake until the mixture is hot and bubbling, about 25 to 30 minutes. Remove and turn on the broiler. Brown the macaroni and cheese under the broiler until the top is nicely browned, about 3 minutes. Serve at once.

pasta with bolognese sauce

serves 8 to 10; makes 6½ cups sauce

When making this sauce, be sure that you have time to let it cook over a long, slow simmer. It is quite delightful to smell it slowly cooking on the stove over the course of a winter afternoon. Bolognese sauce is excellent with all types of pasta, and it freezes beautifully.

2 tablespoons olive oil

2 tablespoons unsalted butter

1 medium onion, diced

3 stalks celery, diced

3 carrots, peeled and finely diced

¾ pound lean ground beef

¾ pound ground veal

Kosher salt

1 cup dry white wine

½ cup milk

½ teaspoon ground nutmeg

2 cans (28 ounces each) plum tomatoes, coarsely chopped, with their juices

Freshly ground black pepper

Freshly grated Parmesan cheese, for serving

1½ pounds pasta, cooked according to package directions

1. In a large Dutch oven, heat the oil and butter over medium heat. Add the onion and cook until just translucent. Add the celery and carrots and cook for 2 minutes.
2. Add the ground beef and veal, crumbling it in the pot with a fork. Add salt to taste, stir, and cook until the meat has lost its raw red color. Turn the heat up to medium-high, add the wine, and cook, stirring occasionally, until the wine has evaporated.
3. Turn the heat down to medium, add the milk and nutmeg, and cook, stirring frequently, until the milk has evaporated.
4. Add the tomatoes and their juices and stir well to combine. Bring to a boil, reduce the heat, and cook at a very low simmer. Cook, uncovered, for 3½ to 4 hours, stirring occasionally. Season to taste with additional salt and freshly ground black pepper. The sauce will keep, covered, in the refrigerator for up to 5 days. It may be frozen for up to a month.
5. Serve warm over desired pasta with freshly grated Parmesan cheese.

chapter 5

salads &
side dishes

side dishes are special and important components of every meal, and this chapter offers a range of savory and satisfying accompaniments that are sure to please. While we don't usually think of winter as a prime time for vegetables, that's not really the case. Watercress, spinach, Swiss chard, cabbage, cauliflower, fennel, and mushrooms are readily available for making delicious salads or baked, braised, or roasted side dishes. Hearty potatoes and root vegetables—perfect for slow-roasting, baking, and mashing—are almost always at the market too. And don't forget homemade biscuits and bread. They are well worth their effort and round out any cold-weather dinner.

endive & watercress salad with oranges & avocados

serves 6

This salad of crisp endive and watercress with oranges and avocados is an excellent dinner starter, bringing the freshness of the garden to the winter table.

½ cup pomegranate juice

¼ cup orange juice

1½ teaspoons rice vinegar

1 teaspoon honey

2 shallots, coarsely chopped

¼ cup olive oil

Kosher salt and freshly ground
    black pepper

4 large heads endive

1 bunch watercress, rinsed and stemmed

2 cups mixed salad greens

2 navel oranges, peeled and cut crosswise
    into ¼-inch-thick slices

1 small red onion, thinly sliced

1 avocado, peeled, pitted, and cut
    into ¼-inch pieces

1. To make the dressing, put the pomegranate juice, orange juice, vinegar, honey, shallots, olive oil, and salt and pepper to taste in a blender. Blend until smooth. (The dressing may be made a day ahead and will keep, covered, in the refrigerator. Bring to room temperature and blend well before using.)

2. Trim off the base of the endives, separate the leaves, and tear into thirds. Put in a large salad bowl, add the watercress and greens, and toss together. Drizzle with enough dressing to coat the greens.

3. Put the oranges and onion in a small bowl and drizzle with enough dressing to coat, and toss together.

4. Just before serving, arrange the salad on 6 individual plates and top each serving with the orange and onion mixture and the avocado pieces. Drizzle each serving with a bit of the dressing and serve.

spinach salad
with warm mushrooms & goat cheese

serves 6

I like to make salads all year round, and in the wintertime, that often means using fresh spinach and warm and woodsy mushrooms to create something appropriately flavorful and satisfying. This salad also gets extra zest from black olives and capers.

5 tablespoons extra-virgin olive oil

I cup stemmed and thinly sliced cremini mushrooms

I cup stemmed and thinly sliced shiitake mushrooms

2 garlic cloves, thinly sliced

2 tablespoons pitted and minced oil-cured black olives, such as kalamata

2 teaspoons drained capers

2 tablespoons fresh lemon juice

I tablespoon balsamic vinegar

2 bunches fresh spinach, stemmed, rinsed, and patted dry

I red onion, thinly sliced

Kosher salt and freshly ground black pepper

½ cup crumbled goat cheese

1. In a sauté pan, heat 3 tablespoons of the oil over medium heat. Add the mushrooms and cook, stirring, 5 minutes. Reduce the heat and stir in the garlic, olives, capers, lemon juice, and vinegar. Simmer for 5 minutes.

2. Tear the spinach into bite-sized pieces and transfer to a large salad bowl. Add the red onion and the remaining 2 tablespoons of the olive oil and toss together to combine. Season to taste with salt and pepper. Add the warm mushroom mixture to the salad and toss again until well blended.

3. Divide the salad among 6 salad plates. Sprinkle with the goat cheese and some additional pepper and serve.

wild rice, apricot, & walnut salad

serves 6 to 8

Buffets are a terrific timesaver for serving weekend guests. This nutty, crunchy salad is great as a part of a lunch or dinner buffet because it complements many types of dishes and may be served chilled or at room temperature. The fruits and nuts add a holiday note to a winter table.

1½ cups wild rice
3 cups water
¾ cup chopped dried apricots
¾ cup walnut halves, toasted and chopped (see page 25)
1 teaspoon Dijon mustard

1 teaspoon red wine vinegar
3 tablespoons extra-virgin olive oil
Kosher salt and freshly ground black pepper
½ cup fresh chopped flat-leaf parsley
1 tablespoon fresh lemon juice
2 tablespoons walnut oil

1. Put the rice and water in a saucepan, bring to a boil, cover, and simmer over very low heat until the rice is tender, 40 to 45 minutes. Let the rice sit, covered, for 10 minutes. Fluff the rice with a fork and transfer to a large bowl. Add the apricots and walnuts and toss together.

2. In a small bowl, whisk together the mustard, vinegar, olive oil, and salt and pepper to taste to combine. Pour over the rice and toss together. Add the parsley and lemon juice and toss. Drizzle the salad with the walnut oil and toss again. Taste and adjust the seasonings, if necessary. Serve the salad chilled or at room temperature.

braised red cabbage & apples

serves 6

Red cabbage braised with cider and a bright green Granny Smith apple is very easy to prepare and makes a wonderful side dish for roast pork or chicken. Its classic flavors are heartening after a day out in the winter's chill.

2 tablespoons corn, canola,
   or safflower oil
1 red onion, thinly sliced
6 cups shredded red cabbage
Kosher salt

1 Granny Smith apple, cored and chopped
3 tablespoons apple cider
1 tablespoon apple cider vinegar
Pinch of sugar
Freshly ground black pepper

1. In a large pot or saucepan with a lid, heat the oil and cook the onion, stirring occasionally, over low heat until softened, about 10 minutes. Add the cabbage and salt to taste. Cover and cook over low heat for 10 minutes.

2. Add the apple, cider, vinegar, and sugar and cook, stirring occasionally, until the cabbage and apple are soft, 20 to 25 minutes. Add pepper and additional salt to taste, if necessary, and serve at once.

stir-fried coleslaw

Warm stir-fried coleslaw, made with fresh green cabbage, bell peppers, and carrots is a delightful, change-of-pace side dish your guests will enjoy again and again. It puts a winter spin on a summer classic. Try pairing it with Asian-Style Pan-Roasted Spare Ribs (page 80).

6 cups shredded green cabbage

1 teaspoon kosher salt

STIR-FRY SAUCE:

2 tablespoons light soy sauce

2 tablespoons sugar

3 tablespoons rice wine vinegar

Pinch of red pepper flakes

2 tablespoons corn oil

2 tablespoons minced fresh ginger

1 medium red bell pepper, seeded, deveined, and thinly sliced

1 medium yellow bell pepper, seeded, deveined and thinly sliced

2½ cups shredded carrots (about 4 carrots)

2 tablespoons sake

2 tablespoons minced scallions, for garnish

1. Put the cabbage in a large bowl and sprinkle with salt. Let it stand for 30 minutes, then drain in a colander and pat dry. Meanwhile, make the stir-fry sauce. Whisk together the soy sauce, sugar, vinegar, and red pepper flakes in a small bowl. Set aside.

2. Heat the oil over medium-high heat in a large skillet. Add the ginger and stir-fry for about 10 seconds. Add the bell peppers and toss for about 2 minutes. Add the cabbage and carrots and toss for another 2 minutes. Add the sake, cover, reduce the heat to medium-high, and cook until the vegetables are tender, about 2 minutes. Add the stir-fry sauce and stir-fry for 1 minute. Transfer to a serving bowl or platter, garnish with the scallions, and serve.

swiss chard
with raisins & toasted pine nuts

serves 6

Swiss chard, which has an earthy and slightly piquant flavor, is a delicious winter green and an excellent source of vitamins and minerals, so it's a healthy cold-weather choice. This quick-cook dish looks and tastes great when you use both white and red chard.

2 tablespoons olive oil

1 cup finely chopped red onion

2 cloves garlic, thinly sliced

¼ cup chicken or vegetable broth, or more to taste

⅓ cup golden raisins

2 bunches Swiss chard, preferably white and red, stemmed and coarsely chopped

Kosher salt and freshly ground black pepper

½ cup pine nuts, toasted (see page 25)

1. In a large skillet, heat the oil over medium heat. Add the onion and garlic and cook, stirring often, until softened, about 3 minutes. Add the broth and raisins, reduce the heat, and simmer for about 2 minutes. Add the chard and cook over high heat, tossing well, until the leaves are tender, 3 to 5 minutes. Add more broth if the mixture seems too dry. Season to taste with salt and pepper and toss again.

2. Transfer to a serving dish, sprinkle with the pine nuts, and serve at once.

baked fennel with blue cheese

serves 6

In this dish, the subtle flavor of fennel is enhanced when baked with olive oil and topped with bread crumbs and pungent blue cheese.

2 tablespoons olive oil
2 fennel bulbs, trimmed
¼ cup bread crumbs

½ cup crumbled blue cheese
Freshly ground black pepper

1. Preheat the oven to 350°F. Brush the bottom of a 9½-by-14½- or 10-by-14-inch baking dish with 1 tablespoon of the olive oil.
2. Cut the fennel into ¼-inch-thick slices and layer in the baking dish. Brush the tops of the fennel slices with the remaining 1 tablespoon of olive oil. Bake for 30 minutes. Remove from the oven, turn the fennel slices, and return to the oven. Bake for 30 more minutes.
3. Remove the fennel from the oven, sprinkle the top evenly with the bread crumbs and cheese, season generously with black pepper, and bake until the cheese melts, about 10 minutes.
4. Run the baking dish under the broiler until the top is browned and bubbly, about 3 minutes. Serve hot or at room temperature.

mashed potatoes
with shallots & garlic

serves 6

These mashed potatoes made with sautéed shallots and garlic are utterly satisfying. They're simply delicious with Red Wine–Braised Short Ribs (page 76) or Spicy Lamb Shanks (page 85).

2 pounds Yukon Gold or russet
potatoes, unpeeled

¾ cup whole milk

2 tablespoons unsalted butter,
at room temperature

1 tablespoon olive oil

1 cup thinly sliced shallots

3 cloves garlic, thinly sliced

Kosher salt and freshly ground black pepper

½ cup chopped fresh flat-leaf parsley, for garnish

1. Put the potatoes in a large saucepan and cover with cold water. Bring to a boil, reduce the heat to medium, and simmer, uncovered, until the potatoes are tender, about 20 minutes. Drain and let cool. Peel the potatoes and return them to the dried saucepan. Mash them and set the pan over medium-low heat for 2 minutes.

2. Meanwhile, heat the milk in a small saucepan until warm. Stir the butter into the potatoes. Add the milk and stir until until completely absorbed. Cover and set aside.

3. Heat the oil in a small skillet. Add the shallots and garlic and sauté over medium-low heat, stirring until tender and golden, about 10 minutes. Stir into the potatoes and season to taste with salt and pepper. Garnish with parsley and serve at once.

roasted sweet potato spears
with honey-vinegar glaze

serves 6

Sweet potatoes have a strong association with holiday meals, but they're popular on any table. Here is a fabulous and easy way to serve them, with an unexpected twist. They are an excellent accompaniment to roast chicken or ham.

4 large sweet potatoes
(about 2½ pounds)
2 tablespoons olive oil

Kosher salt and freshly ground black pepper
1 tablespoon honey
1 tablespoon sherry vinegar

1. Preheat the oven to 375°F.
2. Peel the sweet potatoes, then cut each one lengthwise into 6 spears. Cut the spears in half crosswise and transfer to a large bowl. Add the olive oil and a generous sprinkling of salt and pepper to taste. Toss well to coat evenly and let the potatoes stand for 5 minutes.
3. Put the potatoes in 1 layer on a baking sheet and roast, uncovered, turning occasionally, until they are tender and the edges are browned, about 1 hour to 75 minutes. Transfer to a serving dish.
4. In a small bowl, whisk together the honey and vinegar. Drizzle over the potatoes and serve at once.

slow-roasted root vegetables

serves 6

Colorful and tasty root vegetables—carrots, turnips, parsnips, and potatoes—slow-roasted in butter and olive oil make a beautiful and hearty accompaniment to almost any winter dish. This is an especially good side to serve at a holiday meal.

2 tablespoons unsalted butter

3 tablespoons olive oil

4 carrots, peeled, trimmed, and cut into 1-inch pieces

3 parsnips, peeled, trimmed, and cut into 1-inch pieces

1 large yellow turnip or rutabaga (2 pounds), peeled, trimmed, and cut into 1-inch pieces

4 medium red potatoes, unpeeled and cut into 1-inch pieces

Kosher salt and freshly ground black pepper

1 teaspoon chopped fresh rosemary

1 teaspoon chopped fresh thyme

1. Preheat the oven to 350°F.
2. Put a heavy roasting pan over 2 burners on the stove. Heat the butter and olive oil over medium-high heat. Add the carrots, parsnips, turnip, and potatoes and cook, stirring occasionally, until browned in places, about 5 minutes. Generously season the vegetables with salt and pepper to taste. Add the rosemary and thyme and stir well to combine.
3. Roast the vegetables in the oven until soft when pierced and golden brown, about 1 hour. Transfer to a large platter and serve.

mushroom ragoût

serves 6

This rich stew of mixed mushrooms and sherry goes well with all types of dishes, including roast beef or pork. It's also very good as a crostini topping.

1 ounce dried porcini mushrooms

2 tablespoons olive oil

2 shallots, minced

2 garlic cloves, thinly sliced

1 teaspoon ground cumin

1 teaspoon celery seed

10 ounces fresh button mushrooms, thinly sliced

10 ounces fresh cremini mushrooms, thinly sliced

4 ounces fresh shiitake mushrooms, thinly sliced

1 tablespoon flour

¼ cup dry sherry or Madeira

Kosher salt and freshly ground pepper

1 tablespoon fresh lemon juice

2 tablespoons chopped fresh flat-leaf parsley

1. Soak the porcini in 1½ cups boiling water until softened, about 30 minutes.
2. In a large skillet, heat the oil and sauté the shallots and garlic over medium-high heat until softened. Add the cumin and celery seed and stir for 1 minute. Drain the porcini in a fine sieve, reserving the liquid, and add to the pan, stirring, 1 to 2 minutes.
3. Add the fresh mushrooms and cook, stirring, until they begin to soften. Continue to cook, covered, stirring occasionally, for 5 minutes.
4. Stir in the flour, porcini liquid, and sherry. Cover and simmer until the mushrooms are cooked through and the sauce is thickened, about 25 minutes. Sprinkle with the lemon juice and parsley and serve at once.

cheddar cheese & chive biscuits

makes about 8 to 10 biscuits

These down-home flaky biscuits are simple to make. Just be sure to have all your ingredients ready, and don't overwork the dough when kneading it. These are terrific to serve with soup or chili. Or, for delicious hors d'oeuvres, cut the dough into smaller rounds and serve with thin slices of ham or prosciutto, topped with honey mustard.

I cup unbleached all-purpose flour
I cup cake flour
2 teaspoons baking powder
½ teaspoon baking soda
I teaspoon salt
Pinch of cayenne pepper

4 tablespoons chilled unsalted butter, cut into ½-inch pieces
¼ cup grated white cheddar cheese
¼ cup grated yellow cheddar cheese
2 tablespoons finely minced chives
¾ cup buttermilk, or more to taste

1. Preheat the oven to 400°F.
2. In a medium bowl, whisk together the flours, baking powder, baking soda, salt, and cayenne pepper until well blended. Using a pastry cutter, cut in the butter, cheeses, and chives until the mixture is crumbly. Using a wooden spoon, stir in the buttermilk to make a soft, sticky dough. Add a bit more buttermilk if the dough seems too dry.
3. Turn the dough out onto a floured surface and quickly knead the dough until it comes together; do not overwork. Pat or roll out the dough until it is ½ inch thick. Using a 2½-inch biscuit cutter, cut out the biscuits and place them I inch apart on an ungreased baking sheet. Gather up the scraps, knead briefly, and repeat until all of the dough has been used.
4. Bake on a middle rack in the oven until golden brown, 15 to 18 minutes.

skillet jalapeño cornbread

serves 6 to 8

This cornbread is very moist and has an almost cake-like texture. It's a great accompaniment to soup and chili, and its zesty spiciness warms up any winter meal.

1½ cups yellow cornmeal

2 teaspoons baking powder

Kosher salt

⅔ cup safflower oil,
  plus more for the pan

2 eggs

1 container (8 ounces) sour cream

1 can (14¾ ounces) creamed corn

2 tablespoons finely chopped red bell pepper

2 tablespoons finely minced jalapeño pepper

½ cup grated sharp cheddar cheese

½ cup finely grated Monterey Jack cheese

1. Preheat the oven to 350°F. Oil a 9-inch ovenproof skillet or a heavyweight 9-by-11-inch baking pan.
2. In a large bowl, whisk together the cornmeal, baking powder, and salt to taste.
3. In a medium bowl, stir together the ⅔ cup of oil, the eggs, sour cream, and creamed corn. Stir in the bell and jalapeño peppers. Toss the cheeses together in a small bowl, add ¾ cup of the cheeses, and stir. Scrape this mixture into the cornmeal mixture and stir with a wooden spoon until just blended.
4. Pour the batter into the skillet. Scatter the remaining ¼ cup of the cheese over the top.
5. Bake for 45 to 50 minutes, until the edges of the cornbread begin to brown, the top is set, and a toothpick inserted in the center comes out clean. Let cool in the skillet on a wire rack for at least 30 minutes. Cut into wedges, and serve directly from the skillet.

chapter 6

desserts & treats

dessert is always a welcome indulgence, but since winter food is often heavier fare than that served the rest of the year, it makes sense that cold-weather desserts should be simpler and lighter while still being comforting. Whether you're making a homey dessert like bread pudding or just baking a few batches of cookies for hungry kids (and grown-ups), keep it simple and enjoy!

gingi's pound cake
with raspberry-currant sauce

serves 8 to 10

This recipe is adapted from photographer Rita Maas's grandmother, Gingi. It's a lovely pound cake that's spiced with mace instead of nutmeg. It's delicious with Raspberry-Currant Sauce, which is made with frozen raspberries and currant jelly. The sauce will keep for up to a week and can be used for topping other desserts, ice cream, waffles, and pancakes.

2 cups unbleached all-purpose flour

1 teaspoon baking powder

1 teaspoon salt

½ pound (2 sticks) unsalted butter, at room temperature, plus more for the pan

1½ cups sugar

5 eggs, at room temperature, separated

½ teaspoon ground mace

1 teaspoon vanilla extract

RASPBERRY-CURRANT SAUCE:

One 12-ounce package frozen raspberries, thawed

¼ cup sugar

¾ cup water

1 teaspoon cornstarch

2 tablespoons currant jelly

Whipped cream, crème fraîche, or ice cream, for serving (optional)

1. Preheat the oven to 350°F. Generously butter a tube cake pan.
2. Combine the flour, baking powder, and salt in a mixing bowl and set aside. In a large mixing bowl, cream together the ½ pound butter and the sugar. Add the egg yolks, one at a time, to combine well. Add the flour mixture, mace, and vanilla and stir well to combine.
3. Beat the egg whites until stiff peaks form. Fold into the batter until well incorporated. Pour the batter into the prepared pan. Bake until golden and a cake tester comes out clean, 45 to 50 minutes.

continued

4. To prepare the sauce, put the raspberries, sugar, and ½ cup of water in a saucepan. In a small bowl, whisk the cornstarch and remaining ¼ cup of water together to dissolve. Add to the pan and cook over medium-low heat, stirring, until the mixture thickens, about 5 minutes. Add the currant jelly and stir until dissolved. Simmer the sauce for 2 minutes and remove from the heat. The sauce will keep, covered, in the refrigerator for up to a week.

5. Serve the cake with the sauce and whipped cream, crème fraîche, or ice cream, if desired.

dark chocolate cake

Serves 8 to 10

This chocolate cake is moist and rich, and best of all, it's a snap to make. It's fantastic with or without the frosting. It will become part of your dessert repertoire, and not just in winter.

12 ounces semi-sweet chocolate, broken into pieces

⅔ cup unsalted butter, at room temperature, plus more for the pan

½ cup sugar

5 large eggs, at room temperature, separated

⅓ cup unbleached all-purpose flour

CHOCOLATE FROSTING:

4 tablespoons unsalted butter, at room temperature

½ cup confectioners' sugar

1 teaspoon vanilla extract

2 ounces unsweetened chocolate, melted and slightly cooled

1. Preheat the oven to 350°F. Butter a 9½-inch springform pan or a deep, nonstick cake pan.
2. Combine the chocolate, the ⅔ cup butter, and the sugar in the top of a double boiler placed over simmering water. Melt over medium heat, stirring until the ingredients are thoroughly blended. Set aside to cool. Whisk the egg yolks into the chocolate mixture, then whisk in the flour.
3. In a large bowl, beat the egg whites just until they form firm peaks; do not overbeat.
4. Add one-third of the egg whites to the chocolate batter and mix well. Gently fold in the remaining egg whites. Do not overmix, but be sure that the mixture is well blended.
5. Pour the batter into the prepared pan. Bake until the cake is firm and a cake tester comes out clean, 35 to 40 minutes. Cool on a rack for several hours before unmolding.
6. To make the frosting, use an electric mixer to cream the butter and confectioners' sugar together until very light. Add the vanilla and melted chocolate and beat until smooth.
7. Frost the sides and top of the cake. Cut into wedges and serve.

pear & apricot galette

serves 6

A galette is a rustic French country dessert that has a free-form crust and is less structured than a fluted pie or tart. I like to make this warm and appealing dessert for a casual dinner with close friends.

I cup unbleached all-purpose flour

I teaspoon sugar

Pinch of salt

5 tablespoons cold unsalted butter, cut into small pieces, plus more for the baking sheet

I egg

I teaspoon milk

2 tablespoons apricot jam

3 ripe Bosc pears, peeled, cored and quartered,

2 tablespoons unsalted butter, melted

2 teaspoons sugar

Vanilla ice cream, whipped cream, or crème fraîche, for serving (optional)

1. To make the dough, put the flour, sugar, and salt in a food processor or a bowl. Add the butter and pulse in the processor or cut in the butter in the bowl until the mixture is crumbly. In a separate small bowl, beat the egg and milk together. Sprinkle 2 tablespoons of the egg mixture over the flour mixture and pulse or stir, reserving the remainder. Working quickly, gather the dough into a smooth mass. On a lightly floured surface, pat the dough out into a 5-inch disk. Wrap in plastic and chill in the refrigerator for 30 minutes. (The dough may be prepared a day or two ahead and stored at this point. Bring to room temperature before rolling out.)

2. On a lightly floured surface, roll the dough out into a 9½-inch circle. Transfer the dough to a lightly buttered heavy baking sheet. Fold in ¼ inch of the dough around the outer edges of the circle, forming a rim to the tart, and score diagonal indentations around the rim with the back of a knife. Brush the rim with the reserved beaten egg. Brush I tablespoon of the apricot preserves over the bottom of the tart shell. Put the tart shell in the refrigerator and let chill for about 10 minutes.

3. Preheat the oven to 425°F, with a rack in the center.

4. Slice each pear quarter lengthwise into thin wedges. Arrange the pear slices over the shell in a spoke pattern, overlapping them slightly. Trim remaining slices and arrange them in the center of the tart. Lightly brush the pear slices with the melted butter and sprinkle with the sugar.

5. Bake until the dough is crisp and golden and the pears are tender, 25 to 30 minutes.

6. Thin the remaining 1 tablespoon of apricot jam with about ½ teaspoon of warm water and brush over the pear slices. Serve the galette warm with ice cream, whipped cream, or crème fraîche, if desired. (The galette can be rewarmed for 10 minutes at 350°F, if baked ahead.)

bread pudding
with bourbon-fruit sauce

serves 8 to 10

When I make this delicious bread pudding for a crowd, I always make some extra sauce, which can be made with any combination of dried fruit. It keeps in the refrigerator for about a week, and it's fabulous drizzled over ice cream, frozen yogurt, or pound cake. This comforting cold-weather dessert is simple but decadent.

PUDDING:

4 tablespoons unsalted butter,
at room temperature

12 to 16 ½-inch-thick slices day-old
French bread

3 large eggs

½ cup plus 2 tablespoons sugar

3½ cups milk

1 tablespoon vanilla extract

½ teaspoon ground nutmeg

½ teaspoon ground cinnamon

BOURBON-FRUIT SAUCE:

1½ cups water

¼ cup sugar

½ cup golden raisins, currants, dried cranberries,
or dried cherries, or any combination

2 tablespoons unsalted butter

1 teaspoon unbleached all-purpose flour

¼ cup bourbon

2 tablespoons fresh lemon juice

1. Preheat the oven to 325°F. Butter a 9½-by-14½- or 10-by-14-inch baking dish.

2. To prepare the pudding, generously butter the bread slices and arrange them, buttered side up, in the baking dish in a single layer, so that they cover the bottom of the dish.

3. In a large bowl, whisk the eggs with ½ cup of the sugar until smooth. Slowly add the milk, whisking constantly. Add the vanilla and nutmeg and whisk until mixed. Carefully pour the egg mixture over the bread. Mix together the remaining 2 tablespoons of sugar and the cinnamon and sprinkle over the top of the pudding.

continued

4. Put the baking dish in a larger roasting pan and add enough hot water to come halfway up the sides of the dish. Bake until the custard is set, about 50 to 55 minutes. Remove and let cool on a rack.

5. To prepare the sauce, combine the water and sugar in a saucepan and bring to a boil over medium-high heat. Reduce the heat to medium, add the dried fruit, and simmer for about 15 minutes, to plump fruit.

6. In a separate saucepan, melt the butter over medium heat. Add the flour and stir constantly until smooth. Slowly stir in the raisin mixture and bring to a boil. Add the bourbon and lemon juice and cook, stirring, until just boiling. Remove from the heat. You may also make the sauce ahead of time and warm it over low heat until hot, stirring well, just before serving.

7. Spoon the pudding into bowls and serve with the warm sauce spooned over the top.

port-roasted figs
with crème fraîche & honey

serves 6 (3 halves per serving)

Though figs are frequently thought of as summer fruit, growers in some South American countries have a winter harvest. Here is a simple and elegant dessert recipe that makes great wintertime use of these delicious delicacies. The figs are roasted and topped with crème fraîche and a drizzle of honey. Mascarpone, ricotta, or goat cheese also work very well in this recipe.

9 ripe fresh figs

¾ cup port

6 tablespoons crème fraîche

Honey, for drizzling

1. Preheat the oven to 350°F.
2. Cut the figs lengthwise and trim the stems. Pour ¼ cup of the port into a nonreactive baking dish and put the figs, cut side up, in one layer in the dish. Pour the remaining ½ cup port over the figs. Roast the figs, occasionally spooning with the port, until softened, about 30 minutes. Remove and let cool a bit.
3. Top each fig half with a teaspoon of crème fraîche and a drizzle of honey. Serve warm.

mocha mousse
with fresh strawberries

serves 6 to 8

A simple chocolate-coffee mousse, lightened with beaten egg whites and whipped cream, is a rich, delicious dessert to make your guests feel special. Fresh strawberries, which often begin to appear in markets in mid-winter, are a lovely addition to the mousse.

6 ounces good-quality semisweet chocolate

4 large eggs, at room temperature, separated

2 teaspoons sugar

¼ cup brewed espresso or strong coffee

⅔ cup heavy cream

16 fresh strawberries, sliced, for garnish

1. Melt the chocolate in the top of a double boiler set over barely simmering water, stirring until smooth. Set aside to cool slightly.
2. In the bowl of an electric mixer set on medium speed or with a hand mixer, beat the egg yolks and sugar until pale yellow. Stir in the chocolate and espresso until well mixed.
3. In another bowl, with the mixer set on high speed or with a hand mixer, whip the cream until it forms stiff peaks. Using a rubber spatula, gently fold it into the chocolate mixture.
4. In a clean, dry bowl, beat the egg whites at high speed with a clean, dry whisk or hand mixer until stiff peaks form. Using a rubber spatula, gently fold into the chocolate mousse, taking care to incorporate the whites thoroughly.
5. Spoon the mousse into a large serving bowl or individual dessert bowls or goblets. Chill in the refrigerator overnight. Serve garnished with strawberries.

chocolate-hazelnut dipping sauce

serves 6 to 8

For an easy and festive dessert, dip pieces of assorted fruits, such as strawberries, kiwi, mangos, papaya, bananas, and oranges, and macaroons and cubes of angel food cake into scrumptious chocolate-hazelnut dipping sauce. This delicious sauce is simple to prepare and can be made up to a week ahead of time.

CHOCOLATE- HAZELNUT SAUCE:

1½ cup (16 ounces) chocolate syrup

½ cup chocolate hazelnut spread,
    such as Nutella

FRUIT, COOKIES, AND CAKE:

Fresh strawberries, rinsed

Kiwis, mangoes, and papayas, peeled, halved,
    and cut into ½-inch-thick slices

Bananas, peeled and cut into ½-inch rounds

Seedless oranges, peeled and sectioned

Macaroon cookies

Angel food cake, cut into 1-inch cubes

1. To make the sauce: In a small saucepan, stir the chocolate syrup and chocolate hazelnut spread together over low heat until smooth and warm. The sauce will keep, covered, in the refrigerator for up to 1 week. Serve warm or at room temperature.

2. Place a bowl of the chocolate sauce in the center of a large platter. Arrange the fruit, cookies, and cake around the sauce. Serve with long toothpicks or fondue forks.

oatmeal cherry cookies

makes about 4 dozen cookies

These chewy cookies, made with oatmeal, brown sugar, and tart dried cherries, are a perfect treat to eat any time of day. This recipe is adapted from the owners of Wm. Nicholas, a fine takeaway shop in Katonah, New York. Thanks, Andy and Jeff!

½ pound (2 sticks) unsalted butter, at room temperature

1 cup dark brown sugar

½ cup sugar

2 large eggs, at room temperature

1 teaspoon vanilla extract

1½ cups unbleached all-purpose flour

½ teaspoon salt

½ teaspoon baking powder

½ teaspoon baking soda

1 teaspoon cinnamon

2 cups old-fashioned oatmeal (uncooked)

2 cups dried tart cherries

1. Preheat the oven to 350°F.
2. In a large bowl, cream the butter and sugars together with an electric mixer until well blended. Add the eggs and vanilla and beat until light and fluffy.
3. In another bowl, mix together the flour, salt, baking powder, baking soda, and cinnamon. Add to the butter mixture and beat until well blended. Stir in the oatmeal and dried cherries.
4. Drop the batter by tablespoons onto a lightly greased baking sheet and bake until the edges of the cookies are lightly browned, about 12 minutes.
5. Remove and cool the cookies on the baking sheets for about 2 minutes. Transfer to racks to cool completely.

chocolate-chunk cookies

makes about 4 dozen cookies

What's better than a plate of warm chocolate-chunk cookies fresh from the oven on a winter afternoon? You may need to make more than one batch to keep your friends and family satisfied!

$2\frac{1}{4}$ cups unbleached all-purpose flour

1 teaspoon baking soda

Pinch of salt

$\frac{1}{2}$ pound (2 sticks) unsalted butter, at room temperature

$\frac{1}{2}$ cup shortening, such as Crisco

$1\frac{1}{2}$ cups granulated sugar

$\frac{1}{2}$ cup light brown sugar

1 teaspoon vanilla extract

2 eggs, at room temperature

$1\frac{1}{2}$ cups semi-sweet chocolate chunks

1. Preheat the oven to 375°F.
2. Combine the flour, baking soda, and salt in a bowl and set aside. In a large bowl, beat the butter, shortening, granulated sugar, brown sugar, and vanilla until smooth. Add the eggs one at a time, incorporating well after each addition. Stir in the flour mixture and chocolate chunks. Drop by rounded teaspoons onto ungreased baking sheets.
3. Bake until golden brown, 10 to 12 minutes. Remove and cool the cookies on the baking sheets for about 2 minutes. Transfer to racks to cool completely.

brownies

serves 6 to 8 (makes 16 brownies)

Winter or summer, on the slopes or at the dock, brownies seem to be everyone's favorite dessert, and this recipe is sure to please. These brownies depend on the use of high-quality butter, eggs, and, of course, chocolate.

¼ pound (1 stick) unsalted butter, at room temperature, plus more for the pan

¾ cup unbleached all-purpose flour, plus more for the pan

5 ounces unsweetened chocolate, preferably Callebaut or Valrhona

1¼ cups sugar

½ teaspoon vanilla extract

3 large eggs, at room temperature

½ cup walnuts, chopped (optional)

Confectioners' sugar, for dusting (optional)

1. Preheat the oven to 325°F. Butter and flour an 8-inch square baking pan.
2. Melt the chocolate and ¼ pound butter in the top of a double boiler. Remove from the heat and let cool for 5 minutes.
3. Put the sugar in a medium bowl and stir in the chocolate mixture. Mix with an electric mixer on medium speed until well blended and smooth, about 30 seconds. Scrape down the insides of the bowl with a rubber spatula.
4. Add the vanilla to the chocolate mixture. Add the eggs, one at a time, with the mixer on low speed. After the eggs are well incorporated, scrape the bowl and blend again until the mixture is very smooth, about 20 seconds.
5. Add the ¾ cup flour to the chocolate mixture and mix well by hand. Stir in walnuts, if using.
6. Spread the batter evenly in the prepared pan. Place on the center oven rack and bake just until a thin crust forms on the top and a cake tester comes out clean, about 35 minutes.
7. Remove the pan from the oven and cool on a wire rack for 1 hour.
8. To serve, sift a bit of confectioners' sugar, if using, over the top and cut into squares.

chapter 7

cold cocktails
& warm drinks

cocktail hour in ski country is a time to relax, sip, and taste. It can include classic cold drinks such as Bloody Marys or Mimosas, or festive thirst-quenchers like Pineapple-Orange Sea Breezes or Campari & Cava Sparklers. Served with a few tasty appetizers, these drinks will be savored by your guests. The warm drinks in this chapter are hearty mugs of goodness to warm both the body and the spirit. Serve these winter warmers after a day of outdoor sports, after dinner, or as a nightcap in front of the fire.

bloody mary

The Bloody Mary is a weekend favorite of tailgaters, brunch-goers, and winter house guests alike. Here are a number of ways to serve this popular and delicious drink, using a basic tomato juice mix that may be made a few days ahead of time. Try mixing up a Spicy Tequila Bloody Mary or a smooth version made with aquavit. Either one is as tasty as the classic!

BLOODY MARY MIX:

One bottle (46-ounces) tomato juice

2 tablespoons fresh lemon juice

1 tablespoon Tabasco sauce
  or Louisiana hot sauce

2 tablespoons prepared horseradish

1 tablespoon Worcestershire sauce

Dash of celery salt

Freshly ground black pepper

To prepare the Bloody Mary mix, combine the tomato juice, lemon juice, Tabasco sauce, horseradish, Worcestershire sauce, celery salt, and black pepper to taste in a large container with a tight-fitting lid. Cover tightly and shake vigorously. The mix may be made up to 3 days ahead. Chill in the refrigerator.

classic bloody mary

serves 6

Ice for serving

12 ounces vodka

Celery stalks, for garnish

Fill each glass with ice cubes, add 2 ounces of vodka, top off with the Bloody Mary mix, and stir. Add a celery stalk for garnish, and serve.

spicy tequila bloody mary

serves 6

Dash of smoked paprika
Dash of red pepper flakes
2 tablespoons fresh lime juice
Ice for serving
12 ounces tequila
Lime wedges, for garnish

Add the paprika, red pepper flakes, and lime juice to the Bloody Mary mix and stir well.
Fill each glass with ice cubes, add 2 ounces of tequila, top off with the Bloody Mary mix, and stir.
Add a lime wedge for garnish, and serve.

aquavit bloody mary

serves 6

Ice for serving
12 ounces aquavit
Asparagus spears, steamed and chilled, for garnish

Fill each glass with ice cubes, add 2 ounces of aquavit, top off with the Bloody Mary mix, and stir.
Add an asparagus spear for garnish, and serve.

bull shot

serves 6

A spicy chilled bull shot, made with vodka and beef bouillon, is a very interesting drink with full strong flavor and a nice lemon-y finish. It is said to be an excellent cure for a hangover, and certainly goes a long way in warming up a winter day.

3 cups (24 ounces) beef bouillon

2 tablespoons fresh lemon juice

1 tablespoon Tabasco sauce or
   Louisiana hot sauce

1 tablespoon Worcestershire sauce

Dash of celery salt

Freshly ground black pepper

Ice for serving

12 ounces vodka

Lemon wedges, for garnish

1. Combine the bouillon, lemon juice, Tabasco sauce, Worcestershire sauce, celery salt, and black pepper to taste in a large container with a tight-fitting lid. Cover tightly and shake vigorously. The mix may be made up to 1 day ahead. Chill in the refrigerator.

2. Fill each glass with ice cubes, add 2 ounces of vodka, top off with the bouillon mixture, and stir. Add a lemon wedge for garnish, and serve.

dark & stormy

serves 6

This drink is made with dark rum and ginger beer and has a rich molasses-like flavor and color—so good to drink in front of a roaring fire on a winter evening.

6 lime wedges

1 tablespoon sugar

12 ounces dark rum

Ice for serving

24 ounces ginger beer

Put a lime wedge and ½ teaspoon sugar in each glass and muddle them. Add 2 ounces of rum to each glass and stir. Fill the glasses with ice, top each with 4 ounces of ginger beer, and serve.

pineapple-orange sea breeze

serves 6

It's fun to whip up a taste of the tropics to serve to guests in the winter. Regardless of the cold weather, everyone's mood gets sunnier.

2 cups pineapple juice

1 cup orange juice

¾ cup white rum

¼ cup plus 2 tablespoons Triple Sec

½ cup seltzer or club soda

8 ice cubes

6 fresh round pineapple slices for garnish

1. Combine the pineapple juice, orange juice, rum, Triple Sec, seltzer or soda, and ice cubes in a blender. Blend at high speed until smooth and frothy.
2. Pour into tall chilled glasses and garnish with pineapple slices. Serve at once.

fresh citrus mimosa

serves 6; makes 12 mimosas

Nothing says "welcome" like this festive version of the traditional mimosa. Chill the Champagne and squeeze the fresh oranges and grapefruits ahead of time so the drinks are ready to assemble as soon as the party begins.

12 oranges

3 pink or ruby red grapefruits

Two 750-milliliter bottles Champagne, chilled

1. Squeeze the oranges and grapefruits and discard their skins. Combine the juices in a large pitcher and chill. This makes about 6 cups of juice.
2. Pour half of the juice into Champagne flutes and add equal amounts of Champagne and stir. Serve at once.

campari & cava sparkler

serves 6

Campari's slightly bitter flavor blends very well with bubbly Spanish cava in this beautiful and sophisticated aperitif.

12 ounces Campari

Ice for serving

One 750-milliliter bottle Spanish cava, chilled

Lime wedges, for garnish

Pour 2 ounces of Campari into each of 6 large wine glasses filled with ice. Top off each drink with the cava and stir. Garnish with a lime wedge, and serve.

warm rum raisin cider

serves 6

Warm cider with raisins and spices is just the thing to drink after a wintertime dinner, along with a plate of cookies or biscotti.

1 tablespoon butter

1 teaspoon sugar

½ cup golden raisins

6 whole cloves

2 cinnamon sticks

6 cups (48 ounces) fresh apple cider

12 ounces dark rum

Apple slices, for garnish

Cinnamon sticks, for garnish

1. In a large saucepan, heat the butter over medium heat. Add the sugar, raisins, cloves, and cinnamon sticks. Cook, stirring constantly, until the sugar has caramelized, about 5 minutes.

2. Add the cider and heat, stirring, until the mixture just begins to simmer. Remove from the heat, stir in the rum, and ladle into cups. Garnish each drink with apple slices and a cinnamon stick, and serve.

mulled pinot noir & brandy

Serves 6

This recipe is a unique and delicious combination of fruity Pinot Noir, raisins, cloves, and cinnamon sticks—a sort of ski season sangria. It's lovely to serve as a nightcap.

1 tablespoon butter
1 teaspoon sugar
½ cup golden raisins
6 whole cloves

2 cinnamon sticks
One 750-milliliter bottle Pinot Noir
8 ounces dark fruit brandy or Grand Marnier
1 orange, sliced into rounds, for garnish

1. In a large saucepan, heat the butter over medium heat. Add the sugar, raisins, cloves, and cinnamon sticks. Cook, stirring constantly, until the sugar has caramelized, about 5 minutes.
2. Add the wine and brandy and heat, stirring, until the mixture just begins to simmer. Remove from the heat and ladle into cups. Garnish each drink with an orange slice, and serve.

brandied mocha coffee

serves 6

Brandy-laced, chocolate-flavored coffee always hits the spot. This is a delightful after-dinner drink.

1 ½ cups whole milk

1 ½ teaspoons unsweetened
cocoa powder

1 tablespoon sugar

¼ cup brandy

3 cups hot freshly brewed coffee

Whipped cream, for garnish (optional)

1. In a medium saucepan, heat the milk over medium heat. Stir in the cocoa and sugar until they are dissolved and the mixture is steaming but not boiling. Stir in the brandy.
2. Slowly pour the hot coffee into the milk mixture, stirring constantly. Ladle the coffee into large warm cups and top with whipped cream, if desired, and serve at once.

winter white hot chocolate

serves 6

Rich hot chocolate made with creamy white chocolate is an elegant drink to sip on a frosty day.

6 cups (48 ounces) whole milk

9 ounces white chocolate,
finely chopped

2 tablespoons vanilla extract

Whipped cream, for garnish (optional)

1. In a large saucepan, heat the milk to simmering over medium heat.
2. Add the chocolate and vanilla, stirring constantly, until completely melted. Cook until hot but not boiling. Remove from the heat and pour into large cups. Top with whipped cream, if desired, and serve at once.

hot chocolate
with cinnamon whipped cream

serves 6

Not for kids only—mugs of hot chocolate and a plate of cookies make a lovely end to a wintry evening's dinner party.

CINNAMON WHIPPED CREAM:

1 cup cold heavy (whipping) cream

1 tablespoon sugar

½ teaspoon ground cinnamon

HOT CHOCOLATE:

6 cups (48 ounces) whole milk

6 tablespoons cocoa powder

2½ tablespoons confectioners' sugar

1 teaspoon vanilla extract

4 ounces semi-sweet chocolate, chopped into small pieces

1. To prepare the whipped cream, put the cream in a large mixing bowl. Using a whisk or an electric mixer, whip the cream until it begins to stiffen. In a small bowl, mix the sugar and cinnamon together and add to the cream. Continue whipping until soft peaks form. If not serving immediately, cover and refrigerate up to 3 hours ahead of time.

2. To prepare the hot chocolate: In a large saucepan, combine the milk, cocoa powder, sugar, and vanilla and cook, stirring constantly, until the mixture is hot, about 5 minutes.

3. Add the chocolate and cook, stirring constantly, until it has melted completely. Remove from the heat and pour into large cups. Top with cinnamon whipped cream and serve at once.

acknowledgments

My thanks and gratitude go to:

Rita Maas, for her wonderful food and location photography.

Michael Pederson, for his beautiful food styling.

Phyllis Asher, for her spot-on prop styling.

Michael Pederson and Kemper Hyers for the generous use of their country home for location photography.

Angela Miller, my agent, who helped make this book happen.

Amy Treadwell, my editor at Chronicle Books, for her good advice and her guidance.

Vanessa Dina, also at Chronicle, who was great to work with on the design of this book.

My husband, Lester, and our daughters, Zan and Isabelle, and to my many good friends for their encouragement and advice, and for being such wonderful dinner companions.

index

TABLE OF EQUIVALENTS

The exact equivalents in the following tables have been rounded for convenience.

LIQUID/DRY MEASURES

U.S.	Metric
1/4 teaspoon	1.25 milliliters
1/2 teaspoon	2.5 milliliters
1 teaspoon	5 milliliters
1 tablespoon (3 teaspoons)	15 milliliters
1 fluid ounce (2 tablespoons)	30 milliliters
1/4 cup	60 milliliters
1/3 cup	80 milliliters
1/2 cup	120 milliliters
1 cup	240 milliliters
1 pint (2 cups)	480 milliliters
1 quart (4 cups, 32 ounces)	960 milliliters
1 gallon (4 quarts)	3.84 liters
1 ounce (by weight)	28 grams
1 pound	448 grams
2.2 pounds	1 kilogram

OVEN TEMPERATURES

Fahrenheit	Celsius	Gas
250	120	1/2
275	140	1
300	150	2
325	160	3
350	180	4
375	190	5
400	200	6
425	220	7
450	230	8
475	240	9
500	260	10

LENGTHS

U.S.	Metric
1/8 inch	3 millimeters
1/4 inch	6 millimeters
1/2 inch	12 millimeters
1 inch	2.5 centimeters